Circles of Collaboration

By

Christine Merser & Leslie Grossman

ISBN: 979-8-9899069-4-9 (Print)
ISBN: 979-8-9922189-1-6 (ePub)
ISBN: 979-8-9899069-5-6 (Kindle)

Library of Congress Control Number: 2025902184

Published by Apricity Publishing
Wiscasset, Maine
ApricityPublishing.com

Printed in the United States

Table of Contents

Stories of Circles of Collaboration

Dedication

To THE EARLY COLLABORATORS WHO first found their way to a circle and then kept it alive, century after century, passing its power to each daughter who carried the spark within her, even when history left no place for it to burn.

And to the women of our generation, who instinctively bring collaboration to their circles, gathering together to achieve extraordinary things.

Authors' Note

DURING THE COVID-19 PANDEMIC, RECONNECTING became "the new black." Both of us began reaching out to those we'd lost touch with. Time at home gave everyone a renewed focus on networking. That's how we started our weekly Zoom meetings, reconnecting after twenty-five years. Leslie's PR firm had once served Christine's e-commerce site, the first luxury goods platform, which was valued at $225 million in 1997.

These meetings became the highlight of our week. We were loud cheerleaders, fierce debaters, and connectors, introducing each other to opportunities and resources while carving out time to discuss our personal lives. Sometimes heated, sometimes celebratory, our conversations always centered on advancing women's parity, individual success, and the pathways to achieving both.

Leslie, comfortable navigating male-dominated power systems, and Christine, a maverick constantly challenging the status quo, often saw the road to change differently. Yet we always returned to a shared core belief: true success in business, across all industries, requires an environment where parity exists regardless of gender.

One of our most persistent debates centered on language and the roles that are accepted and rewarded in business. Christine challenged the idea of "leadership" as a model for women, "The workplace is still playing by rules designed for men, rules rooted in power, strength, and dominance. Instead of trying to fit into that system, women should embrace collaboration as the model. Data shows collaboration delivers stronger results than a 'follow-the-leader' approach.

Leslie agreed with the power of collaboration but argued that leadership is here to stay, "Collaboration is critical, but it's not yet a replacement for the pyramid leadership model cemented over centuries of male dominance. For now, there's room for both models, and women can thrive within the current system while driving change from the inside."

Our debates often came back to language, data, and the ways women work best. Networking was another frequent topic. We agreed that no one succeeds alone.

Leslie recently launched her book *Start with Vision*, a guide to building and using your network effectively. Its core premise is that without a clear vision of your future, it's impossible to create a network that will support your growth. Over time, both of us began exploring a new approach to networking. We recognized that circles, an ancient model of collaboration used by women for centuries, offer enormous untapped potential for driving business success today.

One day, after a weekly session, we both had an epiphany. Our own circles of collaboration had been the key to our successes, and sometimes, to our failures. We realized that when we didn't succeed, it was often because we failed to recognize the people in our circles who could have made the difference. We lost touch with some, overlooked others, or failed to nurture those relationships when they could have helped us most.

We also saw the potential to strengthen these circles. Historically, women have gathered in circles to pool their knowledge and expertise, solving problems together. That model remains powerful today.

Leslie's decades of expertise in networking, combined with Christine's out-of-the-box ideas on collaboration as the new model of leadership, have shaped this book. We believe that collaboration, not competition, is the way forward.

The tools for networking and collaboration have evolved dramatically in the last decade. Where we once relied on geographic proximity, college connections, or professional organizations, today's networks are global and diverse. Technology allows us to connect with people across industries and geographies who share our goals and values.

Christine often says, "Demographics used to be defined by geography, gender, income, and education. Now, they're defined by shared interests. If you love pickleball, you can connect with people across the world who share that passion, regardless of their gender, income, or location.

This shift has created both opportunities and challenges. While we have access to more potential collaborators than ever before, organizing and nurturing those connections has become more complex. How do we identify the people who can help us achieve our goals? How do we maintain meaningful connections in a sea of contacts?

Over the past year, we've worked on answering those questions, refining our own circles of collaboration, and seeing tremendous results. Now, we're excited to share what we've learned.

This isn't just a method, it's a movement. It's about replacing outdated, hierarchical models with something more inclusive and effective. It's about recognizing that everyone has a role to play and that true leadership comes from empowering collaboration.

Imagine having twenty circles on your chart, with categories like finance, social media influencers, industry peers, and strategists. When faced with a big decision, you could invite key collaborators to a short call, provide them with a one-page summary of the issue, and gather their insights. The result? Priceless value for you and new connections for everyone involved.

We're using this system ourselves, expanding our circles while tightening our inner networks. It's transforming the way we work, and we're thrilled to bring this philosophy to others.

The best part? We don't know where it will take us. Maybe one day, leader will take a backseat to collaborator.

We look forward to sharing this journey with you.

Chapter 1

The Circles of Collaboration Premise.

AT THE HEART OF MOST great success stories lies the power of connection, genuine relationships that foster growth, inspiration, and mutual support. We built our model of circles of collaboration on this premise. We achieve more when we surround ourselves with people who challenge us, share in our vision, and offer perspectives we might not see on our own. These circles are intentionally curated, not just by proximity or convenience, but by shared values, goals, and the desire for collective success.

Unlike traditional networking, which often prioritizes quantity, circles of collaboration focus on depth and authenticity. They are ecosystems where each member both gives and receives, where trust and reciprocity are paramount. In our collaborative circles, ideas are exchanged freely, support flows both ways, and the success of one becomes the success of all.

We hope you will find that the beauty of circles of collaboration lies in their dual purpose. Professionally, they provide us with the resources, feedback, and connections we need to thrive. Personally, they offer a sense of belonging and emotional sustenance that keeps us grounded and motivated. These circles remind us that while ambition can drive us forward, it's collaboration that makes the journey meaningful.

And besides, it's so much more rewarding, and, actually, more fun, to do it with others.

Chapter 2

Leader or Collaborator?

WHEN WE ASKED TEN PEOPLE what the opposite of 'leader' was, the answer all ten times? 'Follower'.

But what if the opposite of leader was collaborator?

The two of us differ on the state of the word leader and its relationship to collaborator.

Christine's Point of View...

"Leader becomes a term that is obsolete and leaves the English language.

"I've been increasingly disturbed by the emphasis on women becoming 'leaders.' When I speak to women who, by traditional definitions, would be considered leaders, many reject the term. Many of us say, 'I don't lead. I collaborate. I also don't want to follow. I want to be informed and enlightened by those I choose to follow and seek advice from. Everyone contributes their strengths to my pot pie, and together we succeed.

"I think it's time for the word leader to join Blockbuster and Xerox, relics of a bygone era. Let's replace it with collaborator. Perhaps one of the best things we can do for growth and parity is to start leaving behind language, the vocabulary built by men over the centuries, and build a new vocabulary that better describes what will work for everyone. Let's start with collaboration replacing leader."

Red Rover, Red Rover

"I remember playing Follow the Leader as a young girl, along with Simon Says. Frankly, I was bored by both games. I didn't lose because I couldn't follow directions; I went out because they didn't hold my attention. But then there was Red Rover, where our side collaborated on strategies. I was all in. Trust me, I was very bossy about my opinions, and maybe it's my biased memory, but I'm pretty sure I was on the winning team more often than not."

— CM

Leslie's Point of View...

"Collaborator is used in tandem with leader.

"Personal success in the professional world has always been associated with the term leader. In my vision, creating 'a world where gender equality is a given and no longer a goal' requires using the word leader, as that's the term the world understands.

"Underneath that, my true goal is for women to become the leaders of their own lives, embracing self-determination. They should have both the freedom and the resources to explore their dreams and live the lives they envision for themselves.

"Of course, collaboration is one of the most important tools for achieving one's vision, a skill that women have historically excelled at. However, today's world is more complex, and we all need to learn new tools to fully maximize the benefits of being strong collaborators."

As we explored the history and value of circles of collaboration, it became clear to us both that collaborative circles are the ultimate roadmap for success. By organizing your own circles of collaboration, tailored to your goals and needs, you can achieve more, and enjoy the journey along the way.

Chapter 3

'Her' History with Circles.

A LONG, LONG TIME AGO—5,000 years ago, to be exact—we all had an ancestor who was our gender. Let's call her Emma. Family lore, passed down by the men in our lineage, tells us Emma was a gatherer. Her life was about creating a home, raising the children her strong hunter husband gave her, and subsisting on the meat he provided.

Not so much.

Emma wasn't just a gatherer. She was a hunter, a mother, and, perhaps most importantly, a collaborator. Emma sat in circles with her friends and female family members. Each woman brought her unique skills to the circle to help their families grow and thrive. Prehistoric cave art depicts these circles of women, working together, learning together, and succeeding together. Over the centuries, these circles gave women knowledge, courage, inspiration, and support to become their best selves.

These circles didn't have leaders; they had collaborators. Women contributed their individual expertise and learned from each other. Collaboration. Circles of support. Collective thinking and problem-solving. This is how women functioned at their best.

Men, on the other hand, led through force, and still do. Strong, certain, confident, power-based. They created systems where 'follow the leader' was the rule.

Fast forward a few thousand years to the Salem Witch Trials. On one side, there was the fire-and-brimstone of Samuel Parris, preaching fear and obedience from his pulpit. His sermons didn't bring comfort or solutions, just control. On the other side, there were the women in the woods. These healers gathered in circles, sharing ideas, medicinal remedies, and support. They listened, learned, and collaborated to help their communities.

Parris couldn't compete with the women's circles, so he sought to destroy them. We know what happened next. The Salem Witch Trials were a campaign against collaboration, a way to dismantle women's power. It failed in the end, but the damage was done.

And yet, those circles endured.

Women have historically gathered in collaboration, without a "leader" in the traditional sense, to achieve success. The brilliance of circles lies in their equality, each woman brings her knowledge, and together, they solve problems.

Circles work. Not just because of who sits in them, but because of their shape and structure.

Round tables in boardrooms encourage inclusivity. With no "head" of the table, everyone has an equal voice. Studies show this arrangement fosters collaboration and improves outcomes. There's a clear line of sight for all participants, minimizing the hierarchical dynamic of rectangular tables. Even the absence of sharp corners symbolizes equality.

Native Americans have gathered in circles for centuries, using practices like passing the talking stick to signify who speaks. This method ensures everyone's voice is heard, fostering mutual respect and collective decision-making.

Start by identifying the circles you need, categories like finance, social media, strategists, or industry peers. Fill those circles with people whose expertise will elevate your results. When faced with a challenge, gather your circle, present the issue, and invite their input. You'll make better decisions, faster, and build stronger connections along the way.

The best part? Collaboration is reciprocal. By contributing to others' circles, you gain invaluable relationships, mentors, and mentees who make the journey worthwhile.

It's a friendly quid pro quo. And together, we can achieve extraordinary things.

Chapter 4

The Lindholm Høje Cemetery, Denmark.

THIS LAST STORY ABOUT OUR remarkable history of women and circles of collaboration deserved its own chapter. Interestingly, we didn't come across it while researching that history. Instead, a friend, one of our sounding boards as we developed our circles of collaboration method, called us, excited after returning from a trip to Denmark.

"Have you heard of the Lindholm Høje cemetery?"

"Nope, but it sounds old."

She launched into the tale of this ancient Viking burial ground, dating back to 400–1000 CE. As she described the stark, wind-swept hill where stone circles and ship-shaped markers still stand, we were captivated.

"You know," she said, "the women were buried in circles there, while the men had tombstones shaped like ships. Doesn't that fit perfect-ly with the book you're writing?"

She was right. The symbolism is astonishing, timeless, really. Weaving this cemetery's story into *Circles of Collaboration* seemed like kismet.

In Viking society, the circle held deep significance, and nowhere is this more evident than at Lindholm Høje. The women's graves, marked by stones arranged in perfect circles, symbolize eternity, continuity, and the cyclical nature of life. The men, by contrast, were buried beneath stone outlines shaped like ships, symbols of power, exploration, and individual journeys.

The contrast between these burial styles is a powerful metaphor for the roles of men and women in ancient times. Women were the center of the home and community, the quiet yet unbreakable force that sustained life and ensured the survival of the clan. Their graves reflect this continuity, celebrating the feminine strength that comes not from leading the charge but from holding the circle together.

Men, on the other hand, were often seen as solitary leaders, embarking on linear quests to conquer or protect. The ship-shaped graves celebrated their journeys, both literal and symbolic, honoring their role as providers and defenders. A ship, after all, is designed to move forward, to break through waves, to lead.

As our friend continued to talk, the connection between these graves and the themes of our book became even clearer. Circles are timeless. From ancient rituals to modern boardrooms, women have gathered in circles to collaborate, share, and build. Unlike the hierarchical structures that often define male leadership, one man leading the charge, like a captain steering his ship, women's collaboration thrives in egalitarian spaces.

Even the act of burying women in circles at Lindholm Høje underscores this truth. The circle is inclusive, offering no single point of focus or power. It reflects the kind of leadership that builds consensus, strengthens communities, and sustains generations.

By contrast, the ship graves remind us of the male pursuit of individual legacy and outward ambition. There's a beauty in this, too, an undeniable drive to explore uncharted waters and take risks. But it's a different kind of beauty, one that complements rather than replaces the steady, nurturing power of the circle.

The Vikings understood this balance, even if they didn't articulate it in modern terms. The men led journeys; the women kept the home fires burning. Together, they sustained a civilization built on the duality of forward motion and grounded stability, of outward ambition and inward focus.

We realized that this story of Lindholm Høje was the perfect way to begin *Circles of Collaboration*. The graves on that hilltop remind us that these patterns, women gathering in circles, men charting solo paths, aren't just social constructs; they're ancient truths woven into the fabric of humanity.

Today, as we strive for more collaborative workplaces, equitable leadership, and shared power, it's worth remembering the wisdom of the circle. Women have been collaborators since the beginning of time, gathering together to sustain life, solve problems, and create.

The Lindholm Høje Cemetery, Denmark.

Perhaps it's time to return to that circle, not as a relic of the past, but as a model for the future.

Chapter 5

The Evolution and Disruption
of Networking.

JOIN HANDS, AND LET'S TAKE a walk back in time, before the buzz of phones, the hum of computers, and the instant pings of social media notifications. Networking, back then, was tied to something as simple, and as limiting, as geography. Our world, and our network, consisted of the people we saw in our village or town. Our neighbors, our church group, the merchants in the marketplace. These were our connections. Our opportunities to grow or learn were dictated by proximity and chance. We could only build relationships with people who physically crossed our path.

Then, life became more mobile. People started moving from place to place for work, for love, or for adventure. Enter the era of networking organizations. We could join a club or society, be it the local garden club, the Rotary, or a trade union, and those organizations often extended beyond town lines. Perhaps there was a state or even a national chapter we could connect with.

Then came phones, and even television and radio, giving us a wider range of exposure to people and points of view. We could reach out to them and connect, albeit in a limited way. Letters were big back then. Remember letters?

For the first time, we could build networks that weren't limited by geography but by shared interests or professions. Networking was growing up, but it was still constrained. If we didn't meet someone at a conference, a book club, a meeting, or a neighborhood barbecue, they weren't going to be part of our circle. And we met for drinks after work, not just with friends but with colleagues as well. We built a trusted network through these interactions.

Then came the end of the 20th century.

And then, big bang one—the Internet exploded onto the scene. Suddenly, geography was irrelevant. The world opened up. Networking went global, and it was instantaneous. We could "meet" someone halfway across the globe with a few keystrokes. We could join an online group, exchange ideas, or even collaborate on projects without ever being in the same room, or even on the same continent. Our networks could now include hundreds, even thousands, of people. And for a while, that felt exhilarating. Limitless.

We became very, very busy.

Then came the unintended consequences. In our opinion, with such rapid growth, we started to lose something fundamental. The depth of relationships began to fade in favor of breadth. Sure, we could connect with 1,600 people on LinkedIn, but were those connections truly meaningful? Did they know our goals, our dreams, our challenges? And did we know theirs? A network of that size made nurturing those relationships nearly impossible. Suddenly, supporting our network, or seeking their support, felt overwhelming. The to-do list of favors, responses, and requests became longer than our lifespan. The network was growing, but was it really working?

Research supports this observation. Studies show that the quality of friendships significantly predicts well-being and can protect against mental health issues such as depression and anxiety. A review of 38 studies found that adult friendships, especially high-quality ones that provide social support and companionship, have a lasting positive impact on well-being across the lifespan.

Furthermore, for older adults, it's the quality of friendships, not the quantity, that improves well-being. Smaller, more intimate social networks are associated with higher life satisfaction and better mental health outcomes.

And then, big bang two—COVID-19 attacked.

For all the pain, loss, and upheaval the pandemic caused, it also gave us a moment to stop and reflect. Our networks became smaller, not necessarily by choice but by necessity. In-person gatherings ceased. We leaned on those closest to us, our true circles. And while Zoom use (and stock) skyrocketed, the relationships we built in those Zoom calls were different. Rewarding, informative, but different.

We saw the value of fewer, more meaningful relationships. Instead of chasing a wider network, many of us turned inward, appreciating the power of a smaller, more intentional circle. And perhaps, in that slowdown, we started to glimpse what a healthy network could look like.

Now, as we step into this new era, we believe we're entering a period of networking enlightenment. It's not about how many people we're connected to but about the quality of those connections. It's about creating circles of collaboration, networks consciously designed to support not only our goals but the goals of those within them. These circles are more than professional alliances; they're emotional ecosystems. They feed us, nurture us, and help us grow.

So, what does this mean for the future of networking?

It means rethinking how we approach it. Instead of casting the widest net, we can thoughtfully determine who should be in our network. Who inspires us? Who challenges us? Who shares our values and visions? And just as importantly, how can we reciprocate in meaningful ways?

This is the new networking, a practice rooted in intention, collaboration, and true connection.

Imagine what that could look like. Imagine the power of a network that doesn't just grow outward but grows deep. A network that supports our vision, helps us reach our goals, and allows us to give that same gift to others.

That's not just networking; that's life-changing.

As you imagine it, what you are seeing is your circles of collaboration.

Chapter 6

What's Your Vision?

THERE'S A VOICEOVER AT THE beginning of *Pretty Woman,* an iconic film from the nineties where a fairy tale ending for a prostitute took the country by storm. "What's your dream?" the voice asks as the camera pans over the seedier sections of Los Angeles.

Everyone has a dream, right? A dream sometimes seems out of reach.

Before you can build your circle diagrams, you need clarity on where you're headed. What is your vision?

"First, determine what matters to you most. What would light you up every day if you could spend your time doing it? You might have more than one vision, but decide what is the one thing you would focus all your energy on if you had the opportunity.

"Is it building a financially successful company? Or is it creating a company that has a huge impact on people, solving problems, or making things better? Or is it about being creative?

"If it's a nonprofit, how does it change the world, a community, or a specific demographic? It's not just the what, it's defining the results of the what." — LG

A good first step is to ask yourself if you have too many visions. Can you determine which vision matters to you most? It might be building a company. Rising through the ranks to become the CEO of Meta. Providing support and a road map for building a family. Whatever it is, define it.

Sometimes More is Just More, Not Better

"After Leslie and I started to explore this concept, I realized I had too many goals and dreams, and many of them didn't intersect. The first gift our circles method gave me was the ability to pare down my involvement. I love film. I'm a film podcaster. I love women and entrepreneurship; I wrote articles and interviewed women on all kinds of topics under that header. (God, I hate using the past tense, but there you have it.) I played tournament backgammon and co-founded Women's World of Backgammon to increase the dismal female turnout at tournaments worldwide. And then there's my love of writing and publishing my first novel, *Flight of the Starling*, which can be found on Amazon, with two series books following it.

"Final vision? A series on Netflix, fingers crossed. And my consulting business, which has funded much of what I love to do, and, and, and...

"Note to self: If you dilute your focus with so many ideas, each of which could be a full-time job for someone else, you're not realistically assessing your road to success. Your vision isn't clear. That highway will be so crowded with traffic that you'll come to a standstill. So I had to cut everything but the main goal: to be a world-renowned, financially successful writer. I also narrowed my consulting, allowing me to make money helping others while elevating my work to the promised land of world recognition and financial freedom to go anywhere and do anything I choose.

"Following what we have charted here has given me the focus I need to succeed. I can see it."

— CM

And some people have more than one vision. They might intersect, but your circles of collaboration may change depending on which vision you're focusing on.

Leslie's Book on Vision

Leslie has literally written the book on vision. In *Start with Vision*, she lays out a step-by-step framework for identifying your vision, or visions, and creating the road map to reach them. The book emphasizes the importance of clarity, focus, and intention.

As Leslie often says, "Without a vision, your goals are just wishful thinking. But with a clear vision, you can chart your course, set your goals, build your circles of collaboration, and reach your destination."

Don't have time to get Leslie's book? (Mistake. Big mistake.) Here are five takeaways to consider before you read on:

1. Your vision is your North Star. It's the guiding force that shapes your decisions and the circles you build to help you succeed.
2. Clarity is everything. The clearer your vision, the stronger your circles will be.
3. Not all visions are created equal. Some will demand more resources, time, and effort. Choose wisely.
4. Your circles will shift. Different visions require different people to support them.
5. You have to own it. No one else can define your vision for you. It has to come from within.

Your vision is your foundation. Without it, you risk spreading yourself too thin or chasing opportunities that lead nowhere.

Remember: the clearer your vision, the stronger your circles. And the stronger your circles, the closer you'll get to achieving your dreams.

Chapter 7

Expanding Outside Your Comfort Zone Circles.

OH, THE COMFORT OF THE circles in which we play. "She knows me. She gets me. I'm safe here." There's an undeniable warmth in sticking with the familiar, with the people and spaces that validate us over and over again. Safe. No surprises to set you back. No one questioning you in a way that makes you uncomfortable.

As a society, and through things like social media, we have become people who find mirrors of ourselves, surround-sounding our lives so that we are not challenged. Our beliefs go unchallenged. Our paths remain unevaluated by those who might be able to show us something in the direction we are headed that we haven't seen ourselves.

So here's the truth behind the myth, you cannot have a successful circle of collaboration if you stay inside the same safe fences you've built around yourself. Comfort zones are cozy, but they're also limiting. Collaboration thrives on the diversity of thought, experience, and perspective. To grow, we must break the circle and venture into new territory, even when it feels risky.

The Danger of Staying Safe

In business, as in life, the familiar can become a trap. We gravitate toward people who "get" us, who make us feel secure and seen. While that kind of connection is invaluable, staying exclusively within those circles can lead to stagnation. The most successful collaborations are dynamic. They grow and evolve as we expand our own horizons.

Think of someone like Ruth Bader Ginsburg. When she began her career in law, she entered rooms dominated by men who had little interest in hearing her voice. But she didn't let that stop her.

"Fight for the things that you care about, but do it in a way that will lead others to join you." — RBG

By stepping outside of spaces that validated her and into ones that challenged her, Ginsburg not only grew as a lawyer but also changed the course of history.

The Fear of Rejection

Reaching out to people outside our comfort zones can be intimidating. What if they don't like us? What if they say no? But fear of rejection is just that, a fear. And while rejection is inevitable at times, the rewards of putting ourselves out there far outweigh the risks.

We've all had those moments of hesitation. One of us vividly remembers attending a high-profile industry event where it felt like everyone in the room was more accomplished, better connected, or more polished. It would've been easy to retreat to the corner, to stay small. But instead, a simple introduction to someone at the coffee station led to a collaborative project that remains one of the highlights of her career.

But we can also both look back and remember when we didn't take the leap. When we didn't go to that event, maybe because we weren't feeling our most fabulous that year (or even that decade), or because we worried too much about what others might think.

Here's the revelation. Most people aren't thinking about you. They're thinking about themselves.

"I tell my clients all the time, no one cares about you. They care about themselves and what they need to solve a problem or enhance their position in that moment." — CM

Preparation as a Game Changer

"This is where I believe preparation enters the arena. Prepare for the event. Look at past attendee lists. Announce you are going. Put it in your newsletter, on social media, or in a few emails.

"Prepare your intro, a very brief 'who you are' and 'why you are attending.' Ask a few questions. Why did you decide to attend? Who are you hoping to meet here? By asking questions, you'll learn about their interests and be able to share what you have in common with them. That's where the true connection happens. You might leave with a new 'best friend' and a new member of your circle of collaboration.

"As for the speakers, research them ahead of time and decide if you want to meet them after they speak. Don't leave without getting their contact information and sharing yours. Be up to date on the topic. Remind yourself that it's an act of courage to show up in a strange place where you know no one. And courageous acts are the things success is made of." — LG

The Lesson? Step Into the Room.

Go to the places where you feel like the smallest person in the room. Or the largest. Or the least qualified. Growth doesn't happen in rooms that simply validate your presence; it happens in rooms that challenge it.

Chapter 8

The Shape of Collaboration.

CHRISTINE HAS A THING ABOUT the head of the table. Maybe it goes back to the memory of Thanksgiving, when her mother spent all day preparing the meal. Her father would sit at the head of the table with the electric knife in his hand, carve the first slice of white meat, place it on the table, and announce, "Tilly, I think this turkey is the best one you've made. It's moist and easy to carve." He dictated the actions and opinions of everyone around the table, leading the conversation before anyone had even tasted the turkey.

Or maybe it was the boardrooms she sat in early in her career, often the only woman in the room, noticing how people strategically chose their seats. The two chairs to the right and left of the head of the table were coveted. Over and over again, she would arrive early, trying to summon the courage to sit in one of those seats.

"I never took one of them. I sure would now." — CM

When it comes to fostering collaboration, the environment we create is as important as the people we bring to the table. Quite literally.

We believe that assembling your circles of collaboration requires intentionality, ensuring that everyone in the group feels valued, respected, and aware of who their fellow collaborators are, and why they have a place alongside you.

A groundbreaking Harvard study on boardroom dynamics revealed that the shape of a table can profoundly influence the outcomes of meetings. Rectangular tables, the staple of traditional boardrooms, subtly enforce hierarchy. The person seated at the head is perceived as the leader, and the flow of conversation often mirrors this power dynamic. In contrast, circular tables eliminate this unspoken ranking, fostering equality, encouraging participation, and leading to stronger collaboration.

This insight isn't just a modern discovery. Throughout history, circles have been the ultimate shape for gatherings, signaling inclusion, balance, and shared purpose. From ancient times to contemporary settings, the power of the circle has been a common thread in fostering connection and collaboration.

Think about Native American councils and sewing circles. Even Maypole dances, where women moved in individual rhythms that reflected their emotions, created a shared, beautiful vision of unity as the group danced together in a circle.

In the Harvard study, researchers observed teams conducting problem-solving sessions at tables of varying shapes. The findings were striking. Groups seated at circular tables exhibited higher levels of engagement, creativity, and positive interpersonal dynamics compared to those seated at rectangular tables. The circular configuration removed physical and psychological barriers, creating an environment where participants felt equally valued.

Participants at circular tables were also more likely to speak in turn, building on one another's ideas rather than interrupting or dominating the conversation. The absence of a "head seat" equalized status, making room for contributions from quieter individuals who might have felt overshadowed in a more hierarchical setting.

The takeaway? Physical environments are not neutral. Neither are Zoom environments. They influence how we interact, communicate, and collaborate. The shape of a table might seem trivial, but it can subtly shape the power dynamics of an entire group.

Raise Your Meeting IQ

To maximize the power of your circles of collaboration, be intentional about how you structure meetings and gatherings, whether in person or online. Keep this chapter in mind when setting up your next meeting.

Here's our checklist for creating effective, inclusive meetings.

- **Zoom calls.** Send attendees a note beforehand with a sentence or two about each participant.
- **Pre-introductions.** Consider sending an email introducing two people before the meeting so they can make a connection in advance.
- **Name tags.** Sometimes.
- **Round tables.** Whether it's lunch or a meeting, round tables foster better collaboration.
- **Assigned seating.** Sometimes.
- **No one gets stuck in the corner.** Arrange seating clusters to keep everyone engaged.

- **Work the room.** Keep moving. Add those steps to your daily count. No sitting with just one person and catching up.
- **Skip the forced icebreakers.** Truth be told, introverts are in a panic.

Chapter 9

The Art of the Ask.

THERE'S A STORY ABOUT STEVE JOBS that never fails to inspire. When Jobs was 12 years old, he called up Bill Hewlett of Hewlett-Packard—yes, the Bill Hewlett—out of the blue. And yes, that's not a typo. He was 12. He asked for spare parts to build a frequency counter. Not only did Hewlett send the parts, but he also offered Jobs a summer internship.

Jobs often reflected on this moment, marveling at how few people actually ask for what they need or want. "Most people never pick up the phone and call. They never ask. And that's what separates the people who do things from the people who just dream about them."

Do the ask.

This idea is the foundation of this chapter. Courageously doing the ask. It's a skill too many of us underestimate. Whether it's fear of rejection, discomfort, or the mistaken belief that asking for help makes us weak, the result is the same. Missed opportunities for growth, connection, and collaboration.

And we would be remiss not to acknowledge that historically, women have been conditioned to respond rather than initiate.

We've been the ones to answer the call, solve the problem, and fill the gap, meeting the needs of others before considering our own.

While this responsiveness has been a strength, it makes us highly capable and, in our opinion, the best problem solvers ever. But it has also created a pattern of waiting to be asked instead of stepping forward with our own asks.

That has to change.

To build and leverage your circles of collaboration, you must become comfortable with making the ask—clearly, directly, and confidently. Whether it's requesting advice, proposing a partnership, or seeking support, asking is not a sign of weakness.

When you do the ask, you invite others into your journey, creating opportunities for collaboration, growth, and shared success. It's time to shift the narrative. Women don't just answer asks. We make them.

The Queen of the Ask

Both of us know someone who is in the PR Hall of Fame and is honored annually by more organizations than you could fit into a rolodex. Though she has been out of public relations for more than a decade, we both agree she is the queen of doing the ask.

She knows everyone in the world.

Okay, maybe not the whole world, but we promise you she knows everyone you would ever need for anything in the United States.

But that's not even her greatest value. Her true value lies in her fearlessness when it comes to doing the ask. She will ask and ask and ask. But here's the thing. She will also answer any 'ask' you bring to her. Not only that, if you say no (and God knows that's a whole other book we won't be writing because we still struggle with it), she is just as grateful as if you had said yes.

She thanks you and might add, 'If you know of anyone,' or 'if you change your mind.'

Her name is Patrice Tanaka, and trust us, you should reach out to her just to introduce yourself.

Be Gracious in the 'No' and Grateful for the 'Yes'

Learn to be gracious when you receive a no and grateful when you receive a yes. And vow not to take rejection personally or let it stop you from asking again.

Remember, author J.K. Rowling was turned down more than two hundred times when she pitched *Harry Potter*.

And look at her now.

How to Do the Ask Effectively

Now that we've established that people want to help, you have to get organized to do the ask. The key is knowing how to ask effectively and respectfully.

This brings us back to your circle of collaboration. Remember, it isn't just a network, it's a resource. Think about the people in your life: friends, colleagues, mentors, clients. Each of them has unique skills, perspectives, and connections. What could they help you with if you just had the courage to ask?

Take a moment to inventory your circles, where you need help, advice, or connections.

- Who do you know with expertise you lack?
- Who might know someone who can help you?
- Who has a perspective you value but haven't tapped into yet?

Now, ask yourself: what can I ask them to do to help me?

This isn't about being transactional or opportunistic. It's about identifying specific, meaningful ways they can support you and framing your request in a way that's clear and respectful of their time.

For example, instead of a vague, "Can you help me with my business strategy?" you might ask, "I'm working on a marketing strategy for my new product launch. Would you have 20 minutes to share your thoughts on how to improve our social media reach?"

Being specific shows that you value their time and input, and it increases the likelihood that they'll say yes.

Do the Ask, but Don't Waste Time

While asking is powerful, it comes with responsibility. One of the fastest ways to alienate people in your circle is to waste their time. Avoid that.

+ **Do your homework.** Before you ask, know what you need and why.
+ **Be concise.** Respect their time by getting to the point quickly.
+ **Offer flexibility.** If you're asking for a meeting, suggest times that work for them or offer to accommodate their schedule.
+ **Acknowledge their value.** Let them know why you're coming to them specifically. "I respect your expertise in X" or "I admire your work on Y" goes a long way.

Do the Offer: Build the Well for Tomorrow

Asking is essential, but so is giving back. The strongest collaborations are built on mutual investment.

This is where the offer comes in: thinking about how you can help others today, knowing it may come back to you in unexpected ways tomorrow.

Don't wait for them to ask.

Both of us spend time each week reaching out to our circles of collaboration, offering information and connections we think might be useful. Christine is always sending articles, podcasts, and social media influencers for those in her circles to follow. Leslie is the ultimate connector. She'll have lunch with someone new in her circle, and the next thing you know, you have an email from her introducing you to that person because of X, Y, or Z.

Start with Small Acts

+ **Send resources.** If you come across an article, podcast, or book that could benefit someone in your circle, don't just think about it. Send it. Go old-school. Print it out, write a quick note, and mail it to 10 people who might find it helpful.
+ **Make introductions.** Who in your network could benefit from knowing each other? Facilitate those connections.
+ **Be a sounding board.** Let people know they can come to you when they need advice or support.

Think Long-Term

Investing in others isn't just about goodwill. It's strategic. Every time you give, you're adding to a well of trust, goodwill, and collaboration that you can draw from in the future. And yes, we agree, that's not the only reason to do it. The best reason is because it feels great. Ten minutes a day is all you need and it will make a marked difference in your connections.

It's the essence of quid pro quo. It's a recognition that we rise by lifting others.

Remember, giving isn't about keeping score. It's about creating a dynamic where everyone in your circle feels empowered to contribute and supported in their own efforts.

When you give freely, you make it easier to ask freely, and to receive generously.

We had an epiphany while working on this chapter—courageously asking and generously offering are a great balance. Just do it. Be bold. Start the minute you put your circles on paper.

Chapter 10

Redefining Quid Pro Quo.

WE DECIDED TO GIVE QUID pro quo its own chapter. It has become the black sheep of networking terminology. Let's change that.

In Latin, quid pro quo means "something for something." At its origin, it described an equal exchange and was rooted in fairness and mutual benefit. Over time, however, we think the phrase has acquired a darker undertone. In modern usage, particularly in legal and cultural contexts, it often implies manipulation, coercion, or dishonesty.

Think of the exchange between Hannibal Lecter and Clarice Starling in *The Silence of the Lambs*, a film often discussed in feminist studies as one of the best feminist films ever made. If you haven't seen it, you might want to make the time. Hannibal, a serial killer behind bars, mentors FBI agent Clarice Starling as she seeks to make her name solving another serial killer case.

"Quid pro quo, Clarice," he says, in a way that will shake you.

Lecter's quid pro quo was not a fair trade but rather a calculated power play. It's a stark reminder of how imbalance can sour even the simplest exchanges.

But what if we reclaimed the purity of quid pro quo? When approached with mutual admiration and respect, this principle becomes an incredible tool for collaboration. Relationships built on balanced exchanges thrive because both parties feel valued and engaged. Unfortunately, in today's world, the scales often tip, leaving one person drained and disillusioned while the other continues to take without reciprocation. This dynamic, when left unchecked, is a silent killer of partnerships and progress.

Leslie & Christine's Quid Pro Quo

As we mentioned in our introduction, we started doing a one-hour call together during the pandemic.

Leslie is a well-paid executive coach specializing in professional success and fulfillment. Christine is a renowned strategist and marketing guru with a storied career working with corporations, politicians, and entrepreneurs.

We can't remember who suggested it first, but we decided that rather than paying each other for what we knew would be valuable information and support, we would dedicate one half-hour each week for Christine to present her issues and ideas, and Leslie would do the same.

At first, we strictly enforced the half-hour rule. But after that first year? Sometimes it's all one or the other's issues and ideas.

We both come prepared each week. We don't waste a moment of our precious time. And we're still doing it.

In addition, one of us might text the other with, "Do you have five minutes?" And we make it five minutes. A pressing question is quickly laid out and answered with the same brevity.

Watch the dialogue on *The West Wing*. CJ Cregg? That woman knows how to lay out a question in two sentences. Prepare your question ahead of time. Treat the time of your circle of collaboration members with care.

Why This Matters in Circles of Collaboration

As we discussed in Do the Ask, the ability to invite others into collaboration is foundational. But understanding and practicing quid pro quo is just as critical. It's so important, in fact, that it deserves its own chapter. Without it, even the most well-intentioned collaborations can crumble. Balanced exchanges are not merely transactional; they are the lifeblood of trust, connection, and shared success.

A Modern Example: A Cautionary Tale

Consider the story of Susan Fowler and Uber, a case that highlights the importance of balance in professional relationships. Fowler, a former engineer at Uber, brought tremendous value to the company through her work. Yet she found herself giving her time, energy, and talent to an environment that offered little respect or reciprocation in return.

Her infamous blog post about the toxic workplace culture not only exposed systemic failures but also underscored what happens when a relationship, personal or professional, becomes one-sided. It was only when Fowler stepped back and said, "Enough," that the imbalance came to light, resulting in massive changes for the company.

The lesson here is simple, when one party consistently gives while the other takes, the relationship will eventually collapse. A balanced quid pro quo is not just good business; it's essential to sustaining collaboration.

That said, it is never a perfectly equal exchange. In one moment, you give me more; in another, I give you more. But the balance overall? We both win.

Redefining Quid Pro Quo for the Modern Era

Instead of viewing quid pro quo as a calculated exchange, we can reframe it as a dynamic interplay of giving and receiving. When done right, it creates a virtuous cycle where both parties feel empowered and appreciated.

This is not about keeping score; it's about fostering a sense of partnership and shared purpose. The key is to approach every exchange with transparency and integrity.

Ask yourself:

+ Am I giving as much as I'm receiving?
+ Are both parties benefiting from this interaction?

By adopting this mindset, quid pro quo becomes a positive force, not a manipulative tactic.

Practical Applications in Collaboration

To apply this redefined quid pro quo in your circles of collaboration:

- **Set clear expectations.** Before engaging in a partnership, discuss what each party brings to the table and what they hope to gain.
- **Practice gratitude and recognition.** Regularly acknowledge the contributions of others. A simple "thank you" can go a long way in maintaining balance.
- **Monitor the relationship's health.** Periodically assess whether the give-and-take feels equitable. If not, address it openly and adjust as needed.

So, let's reclaim quid pro quo in this moment, and let's use it as the powerful tool it was meant to be. Say it out loud. Say it on the subway. Say it on a Zoom call. Let's bring back its original intent.

Chapter 11

The Difference Between Networking and Collaboration.

We talk a lot about building connections, about who we know and who knows us, and that's important. But too often, we confuse networking with collaboration, when in reality, they are two entirely different things.

One is about making contacts, while the other is about cultivating a purposeful circle. Something greater than the sum of its parts. The truth is, most people spend too much time networking and not nearly enough time collaborating.

Let's break it down.

Networking: The Exchange of Favors

Networking is often transactional. It's built around introductions, referrals, and surface-level interactions. It happens at conferences when business cards are exchanged, when people connect on LinkedIn but never actually work together, or when you reach out to someone with a "quick ask" but without a long-term relationship in mind.

Think of it like this:

- Networking is knowing the right people so you can call in a favor when needed.
- It's attending industry events, shaking hands, and making sure your name is remembered.
- It's being in the right room at the right time with the right people.

Now, don't get us wrong. Networking has value. We love it. We use it. It gets your foot in the door. It introduces you to people who may someday become collaborators.

But networking alone doesn't build the architecture of your business support. It doesn't create. It doesn't innovate. And it rarely leads to deep, transformative relationships.

Another issue with networking and joining organizations is that the common denominator in the room isn't your individual vision and goals, it's the shared mission of the event or organization. That's the starting point, not the blueprint for creating your collaborative circles.

Yes, joining organizations that align with your values has merit, but it isn't the same as curating your own circles of collaboration.

The Superficial Rolodex

Let's say you attend an industry conference. You meet a dozen people, have a few great conversations, and walk away with a stack of business cards. Over the next month, you connect with them on LinkedIn, maybe exchange a few messages, but then... nothing.

Maybe you add them to your mailing list. Maybe you nurture one or two relationships. But when you add up the hours, dollars, and dead ends, was it really the best use of your time?

Of course, you should go to that conference. But before you go, identify who you truly want to meet and connect with. Email them beforehand. Come prepared with insights about them that inspire you. Decide whether to expand the relationship or not after your initial conversation.

Collaboration: The Process of Building Something Together

Collaboration is entirely different. It's not just about what someone can do for you. It's about what you can build together.

Think of it like this:

+ Collaboration requires deep trust.
+ It demands a shared vision and commitment.
+ It doesn't end after one introduction. It evolves over time.

Collaboration isn't just knowing someone. It's working with them, challenging them, and creating with them. It's what Sigmund Freud and Wilhelm Stekel did when they gathered their psychoanalytic circle to debate and refine ideas. It's what the Impressionist painters did when they rejected the rigid art institutions and built their own movement.

It's what happens when people don't just trade favors but combine their talents toward something bigger than themselves.

Networking gets you in the door, but collaboration changes the game.

How to Tell the Difference

Here's how you can tell whether you're networking or collaborating.

Networking	Collaboration
Transactional – "I'll do this for you, and you'll do this for me."	**Transformational** – "What can we build together?"
Short-term – Once the favor or event is done, the relationship fades.	**Long-term** – The relationship deepens over time.
Surface-level – Business cards, LinkedIn connections, quick intros.	**Deeply engaged** – Regular meetings, brainstorming, co-creation.
One-sided – Often benefits one party more than the other.	**Mutual investment** – Both parties contribute and gain.

The Danger of Staying in the Networking Zone

Some of us get stuck in perpetual networking mode. We collect contacts, send out feelers, and try to be in the right circles, but we never actually extract value from those connections.

We've seen entrepreneurs go from networking event to networking event, yet their businesses never move forward. We've seen professionals build massive LinkedIn followings but struggle to get anyone to actually work with them.

Because at the end of the day, success isn't about how many people you know. It's about how deeply you collaborate.

Moving from Networking to Collaborating

If you want to stop collecting contacts and start building meaningful collaborations, take a more intentional approach.

Find People Who Challenge You. Real collaborators don't just agree with you. They push you. They bring different skills to the table, challenge your assumptions, and force you to level up.

Stop Looking for Quick Wins. Networking is often about short-term gains, getting an introduction, securing a meeting, making a deal. Collaboration is a long game. Invest in relationships that go beyond one-time transactions.

Create Together. The best collaborations involve building something tangible, a business, a project, a movement. If all you're doing is exchanging emails, you're still just networking. If you're co-creating something, you've stepped into collaboration.

Commit to the Process. True collaboration requires trust, patience, and commitment. It's not about what someone can do for you today. It's about what you can create together over time.

Final Thought: Collaboration is the Future

In a world where connections are easy to make but hard to maintain, the people who truly succeed aren't just good at networking. They're masters of collaboration.

So ask yourself, are you collecting contacts, or are you building something real?

Because at the end of the day, the most powerful circles aren't made up of people who just know each other. They're made up of people who create together.

And have we mentioned that collaboration is so much more engaging, entertaining, and educational? Data shows that gathering, sharing, and spending real time together is good for our health.

And let's face it—it's just more fun.

And shouldn't building our dreams be fun?

Chapter 12

The Outside Circles of Collaboration.

IN A RECENT SPEECH TO real estate agents, Christine emphasized that while the majority of agents claim referrals are their strongest lead generator, they often fail to stay in touch with clients consistently after the sale. As time passes, this follow-up becomes even less frequent.

"If someone is at a dinner party, expresses appreciation for your house, and then asks if you have a real estate broker to recommend, the answer is often not based on your own experience but rather on the first broker that comes to mind," she explained. "That might be someone you read about recently or a listing you noticed where the broker's description of the property stood out. We don't actively search for answers anymore; we react with the first thing that comes to mind, especially if we're not personally invested in the question."

This brings us to the concept of using outside circles when building your circles of collaboration. These are people you've encountered along the way who are part of the broader landscape of your journey toward your vision. While they may not necessarily be called upon to collaborate, you want to maintain a connection. This ensures that if you ever have something to discuss with them, or if they unexpectedly become relevant to your work, you remain on their radar.

You never know when that connection could be valuable.

Because you must stay in their thoughts to avoid being forgotten, it's essential to maintain contact, even if only once or twice a year. It could be as simple as:

+ Sending a holiday card with a personal note
+ Sharing an article you think they might find interesting
+ Googling them once a year to see if there's a reason to reach out

Organizing Your Outside Circles of Collaboration

Create a separate page for your outside circles of collaboration and categorize it based on areas of interest or professional focus.

For example, Christine organizes hers into categories based on her various interests and business ventures. These include:

+ Marketing
+ Backgammon
+ Film
+ Writing
+ Other areas of expertise or passion

She makes it a point to engage with at least one of her outside circles each month. In total, she has twelve outside circles that she nurtures and revisits throughout the year.

By staying intentional with these connections, you ensure that your outside circles remain valuable resources, ones that can open doors, offer insights, and unexpectedly play a role in your success.

Chapter 13

Lessons from Trailblazers.

HISTORY IS FILLED WITH EXAMPLES of people who dared to step outside their circles and found extraordinary success.

Take Maya Angelou. Before becoming one of the most celebrated poets and authors of our time, she performed in nightclubs, worked as a dancer, and even acted on stage. Her diverse experiences informed her writing, making it richer and more universal.

Or consider Kamala Harris, who shattered barriers by running for offices where women of color had traditionally been excluded.

"I was raised to believe I could do anything," Harris said, "but I knew I'd have to walk into rooms where no one looked like me."

Both Angelou and Harris remind us that stepping into spaces where we don't naturally fit isn't just an act of bravery. It's a strategy for growth.

A Word of Caution: Expanding Without Overextending
While growth is essential, it's not about spreading yourself too thin. Expanding your circle doesn't mean saying yes to everything or trying to be everywhere at once.

Be intentional. Choose opportunities that align with your goals and values, and don't be afraid to prioritize quality over quantity.

Breaking the Circle, Building the Future

Growth is uncomfortable. It requires us to challenge our assumptions, confront our fears, and embrace the possibility of failure. But it's also exhilarating.

When we step outside our comfort zones, we discover new ideas, forge unexpected connections, and become better versions of ourselves.

Collaboration is not static. It evolves as we evolve. By breaking out of the circles that have kept us safe, we open ourselves to opportunities we never imagined.

So go ahead, step into that unfamiliar room, reach out to that intimidating contact, and read the book that challenges your beliefs.

Because in the end, the greatest rewards come from the spaces where growth meets collaboration.

Chapter 14

The Quiet Circle:
Sitting Alone With Your Vision.

EVERY GREAT JOURNEY BEGINS AND ends with one person. Us. In the play we call life, the pursuit of our goals, our visions, and our dreams, we are the main characters. No one else carries the responsibility for our choices, and no one else truly inhabits the space where our ambitions live.

This chapter is about that sacred, often uncomfortable moment when all the noise fades away, and we find ourselves in the quiet circle at the center of it all, alone with our thoughts, our intuition, and our decision.

We often think of collaboration as a web of voices, ideas, and input, a collective effort that propels us forward. And it is. But the truest collaborations, the ones that lead to transformative success, always include one vital participant. Ourselves. There comes a time when all the opinions have been voiced, all the data has been collected, and every relevant insight has been examined. In that moment, the circle narrows until only we remain, and the weight of the decision rests solely in our hands.

This solitary moment isn't about isolation or loneliness. It's about clarity. It's about trust, trusting ourselves enough to know that we've listened deeply, gathered the facts worth our attention, and prepared to act. But before we make that leap, there's one final step. Sitting with ourselves and asking the questions that no one else can answer for us.

The Questions We Must Ask Ourselves

In this quiet circle of one, introspection becomes our compass. The questions we ask guide us, and the honesty of our answers defines our outcome. These aren't easy questions, but they are necessary.

- Am I making this decision based on fear or possibility?
- Does this choice align with my vision, or does it serve someone else's expectations?
- If I knew I wouldn't fail, would I make the same choice?
- Am I hesitating because I need more information or because I'm afraid to move forward?
- What is my gut telling me that I might be ignoring?

Trusting Our Inner Voice

The quiet circle is also the place where our inner voice has the opportunity to speak. This voice is not always loud or easy to hear. It often whispers through intuition, a subtle feeling that something is either aligned or off.

Many of us have been trained to doubt this voice, to lean solely on logic or external validation. But our inner voice is our most loyal collaborator. It has been with us in every moment of our lives, absorbing experiences and lessons that no one else has access to.

In this space, we ask ourselves, what does my gut say?

Sometimes, we find that despite all the input and advice, our intuition nudges us in a direction that defies expectation. We honor that voice. It is the sum of our lived experience, and it knows us better than anyone else.

The Power of Stillness

Sitting alone with our vision isn't about overthinking or spiraling into doubt. It's about creating a moment of stillness where clarity can emerge.

We imagine a lake after a storm. Only when the water settles can we see its depths clearly. The same is true of our minds.

This stillness is an act of courage. It's tempting to avoid it, to rush the decision, to lean on others for validation. But when we take the time to sit in the quiet circle, we remind ourselves that no one else carries our vision the way we do.

It's a practice of accountability and self-trust.

Moving Forward

When we finally rise from this quiet circle, decision made, we do so with the confidence that we've honored every voice, every fact, and every instinct.

The circle has done its job. It has gathered, questioned, and clarified.

Now, it's time to act.

This chapter is our reminder that while collaboration is vital, the ultimate collaborator is us. Sitting alone in the quiet circle is not a retreat; it's a return. To our purpose, our vision, and our power.

When we embrace this moment, we step forward not just as the main characters of our story, but as its authors.

Chapter 15

Put It to Paper: Draw It Out.

HUDDLE UP. YOU HAVE TO draw it. Yes, on paper. Nice paper. Or a whiteboard. Or a notebook.

If you can see it, you can be it.

We need to visualize our circles, keep them nearby, and consistently review them. You can do it simply, channel your inner crafty genius, or even have an illustrator design your circle grids.

Before diving in, here's some food for thought to reinforce the importance of putting your vision and circles of collaboration on paper.

A study conducted by Dominican University of California found that people who write down their goals are 42% more likely to achieve them. Adding visualization into the mix, such as creating diagrams of your circles, enhances the brain's ability to connect with the goals on an emotional level, making it easier to stay focused and motivated.

In 1953, Harvard conducted a now-famous study on goal-setting, cited in countless articles and books. Students who wrote down their goals were significantly more likely to achieve them than those who didn't.

Here's the gist of the study's outcome:

- A graduating class of Harvard MBA students was asked if they had goals.
  - 3% said they had clear, written goals.
  - 13% had goals, but they weren't written down.
  - 84% had no goals at all.

Ten years later, researchers discovered:

- The 13% with non-written goals earned twice as much as the 84% with no goals.
- The 3% with written goals outperformed everyone, earning ten times as much as the other 97% combined.

As the old adage goes, "If you can see it, you can be it."

Neuroscience backs this up. *The Journal of Cognitive Neuroscience* reported that mental imagery activates the same areas of the brain as actual experiences, meaning visualizing your success can set the stage for real-world achievements.

Write Down Your Vision/Goal
At the top of the page. In dark ink.

Start by clearly articulating your vision. What's your ultimate goal? If your vision feels broad or overwhelming, break it down into specific, tangible goals that serve as stepping stones to your dream.

Define Your Inner Circle

Who belongs in your inner circle, you ask? The short answer is that it depends on you.

For us, our inner circles aren't about how famous or powerful someone is. It's about the qualities we have determined are needed to support our weaknesses, motivation, and collaboration.

Here are some of the qualities we identified when setting up our inner circles:

- **Trust.** People you can count on.
- **Experience.** Those with relevant knowledge or skills to contribute to your goals.
- **Alignment with Vision.** Individuals who believe in your vision and support your efforts.
- **Honesty.** People who aren't afraid to challenge you or tell you when they disagree.
- **Accessibility.** Those available when you need advice, support, or encouragement.
- **Connection.** A meaningful relationship or history with you.
- **Perspective.** They know your trajectory and can see what you've done and what you need to do.
- **Humor and Positivity.** Because the journey is more enjoyable with them in it.

But hey, every human is different. Decide for yourself who you want in your inner circle.

And remember this: No one needs to know who is in it.

- If someone isn't working as part of your inner circle, you can remove them.
- You can pare it down if needed.
- You can increase the number of people in it.
- You can decrease the number if it feels too large.
- You can add someone, say, a lawyer, when you're going public on the New York Stock Exchange. Then, you can remove them once the stock goes up tenfold at the opening bell. (If you can see it, you can be it.)

If you don't yet have all the people you need for your inner circle (or any of your circles), that's okay. Your circles will evolve over time, and you'll add individuals as you meet them. And you will remove some.

Build Your Intersecting Circles

Now, move to your intersecting circles, those that overlap.

- An industry connection might also be in your inner circle, so those two circles will intertwine.
- If you have too many circles and people you want to include, keep them separate. Instead of intersecting circles, label each circle with a category and list names inside it.

You will be evaluating and rearranging your circles often if you are using them to your advantage. Your circles are not static; they should grow and change as your goals evolve.

Make time to evaluate them regularly.

Resolve to Connect Daily

Commit to reaching out to someone in your circles every day.

- Send them an article they'd find interesting.
- Ask a question.
- Schedule a coffee or lunch date.
- Simply check in.

C-Cubed: Connections, Community, Consult

This practice is about staying engaged with your circles:

1. **Connections.** Strengthen relationships within your circles.
2. **Community.** Contribute to the success of those around you.
3. **Consult.** Seek guidance and advice from those whose input you value.

Your Circles Are More Than Just a Diagram

Both of us think of our circles of collaboration as so much more than just a diagram. They are living, breathing tools for success.

By starting with our vision, identifying the qualities we need in our collaborators, and consistently nurturing these relationships, we've spent the last year creating a framework that is guiding us toward our goals.

Remember: If you can see it, you can be it.

Chapter 16

Circle of Categories: Who Gets to Be in Your Circles?

BUILDING YOUR CIRCLES OF COLLABORATION means thinking intentionally about who, or what, you include in each circle. Who gets to be in your posse?

From friends and family to co-workers and industry specialists, your circles should be tailored to support your vision and goals.

Some people, like Christine, include resources beyond people, such as blogs she follows and podcasts she listens to. Leslie prefers to stick to humans. Whichever approach you take, remember Christine's words in a speech she gave recently about social media posting, "Sometimes more is just more; it's not better."

You'll need to give each circle, and the people or resources in it, your time. Choose wisely.

Here's a "whet your whistle" list to inspire you as you create your circles. These are just examples. Tailor yours to fit your unique vision and goals.

Family and Close Friends

These are the people who know you best and provide emotional support, perspective, and encouragement.

+ A spouse, partner, sibling, cousin, or close friend who cheers you on.
+ A parent or child who believes in your potential.
+ A trusted friend who gives honest advice.

Professional Mentors, Coaches, and Advisors

These are individuals with experience and wisdom in your industry or field. They offer guidance, connections, and insight, helping you navigate challenges.

Community, Nonprofit, and Professional Organizations

When you are an active member of an organization, be it nonprofit, community, religious, or professional, you will meet all kinds of people, many of whom share similar visions, concerns, and goals. This commonality makes relationship-building easier, leading to more collaboration and the addition of trusted people to your circle.

One example of a valuable organization among hundreds is Entreprenista. A few years ago, Stephanie Cartin and Courtney Spritzer, co-owners of a social media company and former coaching clients of Leslie, recognized the support they gained from being members of entrepreneurial organizations. This inspired them to launch their own organization, Entreprenista, specifically for women.

They based it on a circle of support concept, and in just a few short years, they have grown it to well over 3,000 members.

You don't have to create your own organization, but when you actively participate in organizations that align with your goals, magic happens. The key is to attend events, join committees, or serve on the board. By doing so, you'll grow your inner circle with people who share your concerns and value collaboration.

Colleagues and Co-Workers

Think about those in your workplace or professional community who can collaborate, advise, or open doors for potential connections.

+ A peer who shares similar goals.
+ A manager who advocates for you.
+ A co-worker with complementary skills.

Industry Specialists

These are the experts whose deep knowledge can help you solve specific challenges or reach new heights in your field.

+ A PR professional to amplify your message.
+ A financial advisor to manage resources.
+ A strategist to help you map out your goals.

Creative Collaborators

People with fresh perspectives or artistic skills can help you bring your ideas to life.

- A graphic designer to create your brand.
- A photographer or videographer to tell your story visually.
- A writer to craft your messaging.

Resource Circles

These can include blogs, books, podcasts, and other non-human resources that inspire, educate, or inform.

Christine's favorites include:

- Podcasts on leadership and creativity.
- Blogs about marketing trends.
- Books on personal growth and strategy.

Leslie, however, prefers a strictly human approach. Whatever you choose, ensure these resources align with your vision and goals.

Vendors and Professional Services

You'll need professionals who provide essential services to keep your goals on track.

- Accountants for managing finances and tax planning.
- Lawyers for contracts, legal advice, and protection.
- IT professionals for technical needs.

These people may not be in your daily circle, but their expertise is invaluable when needed.

Social Media and Influencers

Social media is a powerful tool for expanding your reach and building connections. Consider:

- **Choosing Platforms.** Focus on platforms where your target audience is active. For professionals, LinkedIn may be a must. For creatives, Instagram or TikTok might be better. Don't spread yourself too thin. Pick 2–3 platforms and excel there.
- **Influencers.** Include those who align with your vision and values. They can amplify your message and connect you with their audience. Look for authenticity, engagement, and relevance over sheer follower count.

And pick from a variety of platforms like LinkedIn, Facebook, YouTube, Blue Sky, etc.

Investors and Financial Backers

If your goals require funding, include investors who share your vision and values.

And throw in a Warren Buffett or Reese Witherspoon-type, someone who doesn't know you yet but will be thrilled when they finally see what you're building.

These individuals or organizations can be part of your circle, providing not only capital but also advice and connections. Remember, you're not just seeking money. You're seeking partnerships.

Fans and Cheerleaders

These are people who might not directly contribute expertise but who champion your vision and offer encouragement. They are valuable in ways that go beyond tangible results.

Wish List: People You Want to Meet

This is your aspirational circle. Include individuals you hope to meet, connect with, or collaborate with in the future.

Even if they don't reply to your outreach, keep them updated. Send them a note when you achieve a milestone or something aligns with their work. Persistence and thoughtful communication can open doors over time.

Health and Wellness

All our journeys require physical and mental stamina, so include people who help you stay healthy and balanced:

+ A fitness coach or yoga instructor.
+ A therapist or counselor for emotional resilience.
+ A nutritionist or health advocate.

Lace Up Your Boots—It's Time to Build Your Circles

Oh my goodness, you are so close to being ready to start using your circles.

Lace up your boots, ladies. Or sneakers. Stilettos. Or saddle shoes!

Ever wonder where lace up your boots comes from?

For centuries, boots have symbolized preparation, hard work, and resilience for women. Historically, we have been depicted lacing up our boots before heading into work, protests, or personal pursuits.

It's a symbol of determination and readiness.

Now, it's time to put that same energy into building your circles of collaboration.

Stories of Circles of
Collaboration

Chapter 17

Our Earliest Circles: The Girl Scouts.

FOR MANY OF US, THE Girl Scouts was our first introduction to the power of collaboration. Sure, we didn't call it that back then, but that's exactly what it was. We learned to rely on each other, lean into each other's strengths, and figure out how to accomplish goals as a group.

It wasn't just about earning badges. Let's be honest, those badges were everything at the time. Each one was proof of something we'd done, something we'd achieved, and they covered our sashes like tiny trophies of determination and teamwork.

Christine remembers how much those badges meant to her. She says, "Even as a kid, they were part of my vision, a banner draped from my shoulder to my hip, covered in evidence of my accomplishments. But here's the thing. I couldn't do it on my own."

"My mom didn't exactly have the skill set required for things like sewing, cooking, or anything remotely related to the outdoors, which, in the sixties, was what the Girl Scouts was all about. So, I set up my first real circle of collaboration.

"One of my troop mates had a mother who could cook. She became part of my circle for the cooking badge. My friend, her mother, and I did the badge together. Another friend's mother could knit anything. Scarves, mittens, you name it. She tried to teach me, and though I never quite got the hang of it (that badge eluded me), I learned from her patience and willingness to help.

"Camping, though, that was collaboration at its finest. None of us could have managed it alone. Pitching tents, gathering firewood, cooking over a flame. It was an all-hands-on-deck experience.

"At the end of each day, we'd gather around the campfire, an actual circle, and share stories. Some of us were brave enough to speak, while others just listened, but whoever had the floor had everyone's attention.

"We were learning to share space, to give and take, and to value each other's contributions."

It's funny, though. Neither Leslie (who was also a Girl Scout) nor Christine can remember the names of the girls from their troop. The faces are blurry now, though the lessons remain clear.

The Girl Scouts was our first exposure to collaboration. And we certainly didn't think to carry those relationships forward. Imagine if we had. Imagine if one or two of those girls were still in our lives, part of our circles now.

High School: New Circles, Same Lessons

High school was another place where circles of collaboration emerged, though in a different way. Maybe your cheerleading squad was one of your circles, full of spirit, laughter, and late-night cheeseburgers on Fridays. Then there was the classmate who always paired with you for science projects, maybe because you both wanted that A, or maybe because you just worked well together. You lost touch after graduation, but in those moments, the two of you were unstoppable. And sometimes, those circles intersected. Maybe your cheerleader best friend became your go-to for advice on big decisions, like where to go to college.

College: Expanding the Circle

College brought even more circles, like study groups, roommates, and club members. People who supported you, challenged you, and helped you grow. And then there was the teacher or professor who saw something in you, something you didn't quite see in yourself. Maybe they encouraged you to take that tough course, pushed you to write that paper, or told you to apply for that internship. And then you left college or high school without saying goodbye, promising yourself you'd reach out someday.

Someday never came.

Reconnecting With the Past

Guess what? Those people are still out there.

We're all easier to find these days. Maybe now is the time to reconnect.

Look back at those early circles and the qualities that drew you to those people in the first place:

- Who knew how to encourage you?
- Who made you laugh?
- Who pushed you to be better?

That professor or teacher who wrote "You can do more" in the margin of your paper might just be the person to remind you of what you're capable of today.

Those qualities that mattered then might be just what you need now as you move forward.

The Foundation for the Future

The truth is, these earliest circles, whether around a campfire, a high school science lab, or a college lecture hall, gave us the foundation for everything that came after.

They taught us to:

- **Collaborate**
- **Trust**
- **Build something greater together**

And while we didn't always carry those relationships forward, the lessons are still with us.

A Chance to Be Intentional

Now, as adults, we have the chance to be more intentional, to recognize the power of those early circles, to reach out and reconnect, and to create new ones that will carry us through the next chapter of our lives.

The seeds were planted back then, sitting in those circles, sharing laughter and stories, leaning on the wisdom of a teacher, or learning the value of teamwork.

All we have to do now is tend to them.

And maybe even reach back to where it all began.

Who knows what you might rediscover?

Maybe it's time to pick up the phone, send that email, or look someone up.

Because those earliest circles, as distant as they may seem, still have the power to shape our future.

Chapter 18

The Exceptions to the Rule:
Martha Stewart & Anna Wintour.

"I met Anna Wintour early in my career when I was doing PR for a hot young fashion designer. She came to the showroom to choose some clothes to feature in her fashion column editorial. She was the fashion editor for Viva, an erotic magazine for women created by the UK publisher of Penthouse Magazine. I remember her clearly because unlike most editors, Wintour was icy cold and aloof and wore dark sunglasses, which became her trademark. She could see out, but you couldn't see in. I recall thinking, "I hope I never have to deal with her again."

— LG

WE RECENTLY WATCHED THE MARTHA STEWART documentary on Netflix. Should we throw the book out? We have worked on our own circles of collaboration for the last few years and this book for at least one year. WTF?

Then we realized something important. We saw that there are exceptions to every single rule. And there's value in studying, and even mirroring, some of the things that make those exceptions successful.

So, we give you Martha Stewart and Anna Wintour, two women who, against all odds, built empires without a circle of collaboration as we define it. And yes, we'd love to have lunch with them. Maybe we could be the exceptions to their rules.

Success Without a Circle?

When we thought of success, especially for women pursuing bold visions, we came to believe it had to be through a circle of collaboration, a tight-knit group of allies, mentors, and supporters who guide, challenge, and celebrate one another. We still think that, for most of us, it's true. And it's a much more gratifying journey than climbing to the top alone.

But after studying these two women, we've gained a new admiration for their journey, even though it will never be ours. Martha Stewart and Anna Wintour defy the norm. They operate in a solitary sphere, driven by an unshakable vision and an extraordinary sense of purpose. Both are icons in their fields. Both are trailblazers. And both have succeeded in ways that challenge the very notion of collaboration. Their stories aren't just fascinating. They reveal that while collaboration can enrich our journeys, it's not the only path to success.

Martha Stewart: The Solitary Visionary

Martha Stewart's rise to the top is the stuff of legend. A self-made mogul, she built an empire around home and lifestyle, redefining how we think about everything from cooking to gardening. But what's striking about her story, as highlighted in her recent documentary, is the almost complete absence of close friends or collaborators.

Martha seems to stand alone in her narrative. There's no tight circle of confidantes or mentors cheering her on. Instead, there's an unwavering certainty, a belief in her own vision and abilities that fueled her through every challenge. She didn't need others to validate her ideas; she knew they were good. Actually, we could argue that she never even showed interest in the ideas of others. Maybe her perseverance and relentless work ethic were her inner circle.

But this solitary approach comes at a cost. Her fall from grace during her legal troubles in the early 2000s showed just how isolating her path had been. Few people stepped up publicly to defend her or offer support. If the documentary is accurate, she shouldn't have gone to jail. If she'd had a circle of collaboration, could she have avoided it? She weathered the storm largely alone. And yet, her resilience and eventual comeback are a testament to the power of sheer determination.

Her comeback also includes an unlikely collaboration, and dare we say, friend? Snoop Dogg. Yes, you heard us correctly. Who would have thought? But together, they've cultivated a multi-generational following on social media, elevating both their brands. And when you see them in the documentary, ask yourself: Do Martha's smiles when she's bantering with him seem... richer?

Martha Stewart said, "As I reflect on my recent collaboration with Snoop, I realize I learn so much from him every time we work together. He's taught me about music and business and always gives me a fresh perspective. We both help each other in that way."

Author's Note: Having diverse individuals who you might not necessarily gravitate to from common interest is not to be ignored when putting together your circles.

Anna Wintour: The Singular Leader

Anna Wintour is our other exception. The iconic editor-in-chief of Vogue and Chief Content Officer of Condé Nast, she operates outside our model of collaboration. She is defined by her singular vision. She doesn't rely on a collaborative circle to shape her ideas; instead, she dictates trends and sets the tone for an entire industry.

Her relationships are professional and transactional, not deeply personal. People admire her from afar, and many work under her direction, but few would describe her as approachable or collaborative. Her leadership style, famously depicted in *The Devil Wears Prada*, reinforces her image as a solitary figure, someone who makes decisions with unwavering confidence, often without consulting others.

Like Martha, Anna inspires admiration more than intimacy. Her influence is undeniable, but it's built on authority and expertise rather than emotional connection. She has long-term, loyal teams, though. Martha, not so much. We can't figure out why that difference exists, but maybe we'll explore it in our next book.

Anna Wintour & Grace Mirabella

There's an anecdote about Anna Wintour that says, during a meeting with her new boss at Vogue, Grace Mirabella (who was then the queen of fashion journalism the way Anna is today), she was asked what job she wanted at the magazine. Anna reportedly replied, "Yours." The meeting ended abruptly. A few months later, Grace was fired, and Anna had the job.

The Power of Certainty

Maybe what sets Stewart and Wintour apart is their extraordinary certainty. They don't question their vision. They don't wait for others to agree with them. They aren't interested in your vision. They are, however, interested in you executing what you're tasked with at the same level of excellence they bring to the table every day.

This clarity of purpose allows them to act decisively and boldly, even in the face of criticism or doubt. For most of us, collaboration provides the feedback and validation we need to move forward. But for Stewart and Wintour? That validation comes from within. Their success proves that confidence and conviction can be just as powerful as collaboration.

The Cost of Solitude

While their paths are inspiring, they also reveal the downsides of going it alone. Both have faced intense scrutiny and challenges. Martha during her legal troubles, and Anna during periods of industry upheaval. Without strong personal networks, those challenges can feel even more isolating for people like us.

And yet, for Stewart and Wintour, solitude seems to fuel their creativity and drive. They thrive in their autonomy, finding strength in independence rather than in a collaborative circle.

Lessons We Can Take from Martha & Anna

Certainty is a superpower. Martha and Anna show us the value of believing deeply in ourselves. Their unshakable confidence allowed them to create groundbreaking legacies. Don't lose your certainty by getting too much input, or input from those without your vision.

Influence can be built from afar. Both Anna and Martha inspire admiration and respect without relying on close personal relationships.

The path is personal. For most of us, collaboration and connection are vital to both personal and professional growth. For them? Not so much.

The Rule and Its Rare Exceptions

For every Martha Stewart or Anna Wintour, there are countless women who have thrived by leaning on circles of collaboration, drawing strength and inspiration from others. So, do Martha and Anna disprove our premise? No.

They simply remind us that success can take many forms. And that sometimes, the exception to the rule… is just as fascinating as the rule itself.

Be So Good

Steve Martin, when asked how he achieved success across comedy, writing, acting, directing, and even banjo playing, famously said, "Be so good they can't ignore you." He noted that people were often disappointed by his answer, expecting advice like making connections with powerful people.

Both Anna Wintour and Steve Martin epitomize this idea. They are so exceptionally good at what they do, they simply can't be ignored.

Chapter 19

COVID-19 Response: Women Prime Ministers Save the Day.

WHEN THE COVID-19 PANDEMIC BROKE out, maybe for the first time, the entire world faced the same crisis. Each country handled it differently. We were stunned when we looked at the standout results of the women-led countries, who took a more collaborative approach to the crisis. If ever there was a model for why collaboration beats "follow the leader," the COVID-19 response is it.

Some countries stood out, not only for their success in managing the pandemic but for the way their leaders approached decision-making. Prime Ministers like Jacinda Ardern of New Zealand and Erna Solberg of Norway exemplified a circles of collaboration style that prioritized inclusivity over hierarchy. Their responses offer a stunning case study in how circles of collaboration can outperform traditional, top-down leadership structures during times of crisis.

Jacinda Ardern: The Power of Collective Expertise

New Zealand's Prime Minister, Jacinda Ardern, garnered widespread praise for her swift, empathetic, and inclusive approach to the pandemic. Rather than centralizing all decisions within a rigid hierarchy, Ardern fostered a collaborative environment where experts in fields such as public health, scientific research, logistics, and communications were empowered to lead within their areas of expertise.

She relied on epidemiologists and medical professionals to guide critical decisions on lockdowns, testing, and vaccinations, ensuring these actions were grounded in science without interference from political agendas. Economists and community leaders were tasked with creating tailored financial aid and recovery strategies, while Ardern herself took the lead in transparent communication, delivering frequent, empathetic updates that kept New Zealanders informed and unified.

By distributing decision-making power to specialists and maintaining respect for their expertise, Ardern's government fostered a spirit of trust and shared responsibility, keeping New Zealand's pandemic response agile, cohesive, and highly effective.

Erna Solberg: Elevating All Voices, Even the Smallest Ones

In Norway, Prime Minister Erna Solberg adopted a similarly collaborative approach, leveraging her government's network of experts and agencies. Solberg emphasized decentralized problem-solving, empowering specialists in public health, logistics, and education to make critical decisions.

One of her most notable strategies was addressing children directly during televised press conferences. Recognizing the fear and confusion children were experiencing, she treated their concerns with respect and importance, demonstrating the collaborative principle of valuing all voices, even those traditionally excluded from decision-making.

Solberg's leadership also encouraged cross-sector collaboration. The health ministry worked closely with education leaders to determine how and when schools could reopen safely, while economists and industry leaders coordinated strategies to maintain employment and support vulnerable populations. Norway's strong culture of social trust enabled her government to delegate responsibilities effectively, avoiding conflicts between overlapping areas of expertise.

The results were clear: Norway maintained one of the lowest infection and mortality rates in Europe while avoiding the political divisions that undermined other countries' responses.

The Contrast: When Hierarchy Fails

Compare this to other countries, including the United States, where pandemic decision-making followed a traditional hierarchical model. Authority was concentrated at the top, with decisions filtering down through layers of bureaucracy.

This approach often resulted in bottlenecks, delayed actions, and conflicts between political priorities and scientific advice. The erosion of public trust led to inconsistent policies and widespread confusion. By contrast, the circle of collaboration model embraced by Ardern and Solberg enabled faster, more coordinated responses with less friction between sectors.

Empowering experts to act decisively within their domains fostered innovation and adaptability, qualities that were essential during a rapidly evolving crisis.

Lessons in Leadership: The Power of Collaboration

The successes of Ardern and Solberg are real-life proof of the power of a collaborative approach to governing. Their leadership was built on four key principles:

1. **Decentralized decision-making** that trusts experts to act independently within their areas of expertise.
2. **Mutual respect among leaders and specialists**, even when decisions intersect across domains.
3. **Transparent communication** to build trust and alignment among stakeholders.
4. **Empathy and inclusion**, prioritizing the needs and voices of all members of society.

These principles not only strengthened their nations' pandemic responses but also demonstrated how circles of collaboration can produce better outcomes and foster stronger public trust.

New Zealand and Norway emerged as global models for effective crisis management, not just because of the outcomes they achieved, but because of how those outcomes were realized. Their approach exemplifies that true leadership is not about commanding from the top; it is about empowering others to lead.

Why Didn't This Change Everything?

You know what slays us? Why didn't this change the way countries, corporations, and organizations approach hierarchy?

If ever there was a clear example of why the old, antiquated pyramid structure of "leadership" doesn't work, this moment in history was it.

Yet, after all the overwhelming evidence, many institutions remain stubbornly loyal to outdated models. Why? Fear of change? Ego? Inertia?

Whatever the reason, the lesson remains clear. Collaboration is not just a feel-good concept, it's a proven model for better outcomes. The question is whether we will ever fully embrace it.

Chapter 20

Christine Merser.

WHEN I FIRST STARTED USING circles of collaboration to approach my strategy for success, I had a lesson to learn before I could put it into action. As I began putting my vision (and goals) to paper and setting up the circles, I realized I had too many goals, too many projects, too many passions. I was just too too. That's the only way to say it.

I have spent considerable time over the past several years weeding out some of what I wanted to do and be. I guess, in the end, my best hope for the future is that we come back to earth again and get to do what we didn't have time for this time around.

But I do have a few separate circles of collaboration charts.

I am an author. Writing that still makes me worry that I'm stating an exaggerated version of what I actually am. But if I can be successful in just one place, and I think we can all agree that being the Chrissie Evert of my time playing tennis has passed, it would be as a writer. Pulitzer? Sure, that would be great, but either way, I am an author.

I write a memoir blog on Substack. I have my first novel out, the first of a three-volume series, *Flight of the Starling*. Do you have time for a plug? It's about a wealthy divorcée who lives a privileged but unfulfilled life and has the opportunity to take part in a black ops mission in the Middle East to save the daughter of her billionaire friend, who was trafficked two decades earlier.

If you think you get to the promised land by writing a one-line description of your novel in another book you're writing for women in business about collaboration, you're not getting the picture. No matter who publishes you, your success is based on your efforts, some luck, and the efforts of others.

Here is my vision. The book will be an international bestseller, and the series, coming out in 2027 on Apple TV+, will have me walking the red carpet, smiling, thinner than I am today, but also sure-footed and not rushing.

My circles are ever-changing as I go on this journey.

I started with people I knew for my inner circle:

+ A lawyer friend.
+ The head of Women in Film & Video New England.
+ Someone who loves my writing and lives in the world my protagonist, Justine, lives: Palm Beach.
+ Another writer further along in her career than me. But quid pro quo, I've helped her a lot in the past.
+ A friend who gets me.

Then I created categories:

- **Film Industry.** People in the film/TV industry. Yes, I have women who are titans, like Reese Witherspoon. While I don't have access to her (*yet*), I follow her and make sure I know what she's up to so that if I can tag in, I will.
- **Book Industry.** People I know or wish I knew who are decision-makers around books.
- **Independent Bookstores.** I've targeted 100 bookstores where I think my book would fit just fine in their window.
- **Book Clubs.** Targeted clubs to approach.
- **Authors.** Authors I know (and some I don't) who have written books similar to mine or in my style. Authors whose books I like.
- **Influencers.** Social media has been great. I engage with them consistently and have pared down those I'm targeting to 20.
- **Resources.** Websites or podcasts. I've whittled it down to five but only listen to maybe two a week.
- **Toolbox.** This category isn't specific to my book hitting the *New York Times* bestseller list but includes tools to help me get closer to my promised land. It might be someone in finance to help me be smarter about money or a marketing person who's brilliant, interesting, and funny.
- **Films and Books.** If there's a film about trafficking, I'm there. I started reading Jean Sasson's *Princess* series (Saudi Arabian princesses imprisoned by their father, based on a real family). I'll write to her when I'm ready, maybe after the second book in my series comes out. I track her on Google so that any article mentioning her name goes to my inbox. I spend 15 minutes weekly reading articles about people

in my circles of collaboration, and it's a game-changer. I've learned about people I never would have known or found book reviewers I should contact.

You get the picture.

I also make a weekly commitment to act in each category to move me closer to my goals. I call it my CM Bingo Card. I print it out, put it on the wall, and check boxes when I complete an outreach. It's printed on Sunday mornings, and by the end of the week, I sometimes scramble to cross off items. Okay, once or twice I've crossed off a box when I shouldn't have, and one week while traveling, my card wasn't great. Progress, not perfection. But it helps.

Having it prominently displayed instead of in a drawer makes it even better. Out of sight, out of mind.

I've removed many people from my circles over the past 12 months as we prepared for the launch of *Flight of the Starling*. I added people, too. And if I add someone, I have to remove someone. I put the removed person in another circle and review it at the end of the year to see if they should come back to me.

I also connect people in the circles. If I hear a great podcast, I look at my circles and share it with someone who might find it relevant. I introduce people who I think should know each other. Rarely, though, and I always ask first and discuss the why I think they should connect.

I do the ask, which isn't easy for me. It's the hardest part of the entire process. I never do it without sleeping on it and ensuring I'm thorough, succinct, and appreciative. Sometimes I call. Sometimes I email. It depends. But if I need something from someone and there's someone in one of my circles who could help, I make myself do the ask. And I have found they will ask back and be grateful for the natural flow of the quid pro quo we have both created.

My bingo card includes blind outreach each week, where I reach out to someone who doesn't know me with a compelling, authentic message. I don't ask for anything but express appreciation for something they did, wrote, or said that moved me.

I'm a work in progress, but the roadmap my circles have laid out for me is working.

Oh happy day!

Chapter 21

Brandi Carlile: Authentic Collaborator.

BRANDI CARLILE IS NOT JUST a musician; she's a connector. Her ability to collaborate with some of the most iconic figures in music, crossing genres from country to rock to folk and spanning generations, has helped her carve out a unique space in the industry. But Carlile's success isn't just about leveraging others' followings to build her own. Her collaborations are rooted in authenticity and mutual respect. One of the central tenets of collaboration is giving back to those who bring value to you. She doesn't just borrow from the spotlight of her collaborators. She shines it back on them, introducing her audience to their work in return.

Collaborating Across Genres

Brandi Carlile's career is a masterclass in using collaboration as a bridge to new audiences. From singing with Elton John to performing with Dolly Parton, Joni Mitchell, and Chris Stapleton, Carlile has seamlessly integrated herself into a lineage of legendary artists. Her collaborations have helped her reach fans who might not have discovered her otherwise, but what makes her approach unique is how she uses her own platform to give back to her collaborators.

One of the most poignant examples of this is her relationship with Joni Mitchell. When Carlile helped organize and perform at Mitchell's surprise return to the stage at the 2022 Newport Folk Festival, she didn't just share Mitchell's legendary status with her audience. She introduced Mitchell to a new generation of fans.

"She's not just a collaborator; she's a steward of music history," said Mitchell. "Brandi makes you feel like you're part of something bigger than just a song."

In doing so, Carlile not only elevated herself through association with Mitchell's iconic career but also helped reintroduce Mitchell's work to a younger, diverse audience through her own devoted fan base.

Quid Pro Quo at Its Best

Carlile's authenticity is the secret sauce that makes her collaborations work. She approaches each partnership with genuine admiration and a willingness to share the spotlight. This is evident in her work with The Highwomen, the country supergroup she co-founded with Maren Morris, Amanda Shires, and Natalie Hemby. The group's goal was to elevate women in country music, a genre often criticized for its lack of gender representation.

In forming The Highwomen, Carlile brought her audience from folk and Americana into country music, introducing them to her collaborators. At the same time, she gained visibility among fans of her bandmates. This wasn't just a business move; it was a heartfelt effort to create a platform where they could all thrive together.

"The Highwomen is about amplifying each other," Carlile said in an interview. "We all bring something unique to the table, and the more we share with each other's fans, the stronger we get as a group."

Carlile doesn't just lean on others' followings. She actively ensures that her collaborators receive as much value as she does. This reciprocal approach to collaboration has built lasting relationships and an ever-expanding audience that respects her authenticity.

The Tenet: Giving Back to Those Who Bring Value

Carlile's ethos of giving back is perhaps best exemplified by her work with smaller, emerging artists. She frequently features them in her shows, brings them on tour, and introduces them to her audience through social media and personal endorsements.

One notable example is when she championed the work of Brittany Howard, the powerhouse vocalist of Alabama Shakes. Carlile praised Howard's artistry in interviews, collaborated with her on stage, and used her own platform to elevate Howard's already rising star.

"When Brandi gives you her platform, she does it fully," Howard said. "She wants her fans to love you the way she does, and it's always genuine. You can tell it's not just about the music. It's about building community."

By uplifting emerging artists, Carlile ensures that collaboration isn't just transactional; it's transformational.

Reciprocity: Not Just a Strategy

This reciprocity isn't just a strategy; it's a reflection of who Carlile is as an artist and a person. Her authenticity builds trust, deepens relationships, and creates an atmosphere where collaboration feels less like a business decision and more like a shared celebration of music.

"Collaboration isn't about what you can take," Carlile once said. "It's about what you can give. When you do it right, everyone rises together."

Through her collaborative spirit, Carlile has not only expanded her own career but has also elevated those around her, showing that the best circles of collaboration are built on authenticity, respect, and mutual uplift.

Chapter 22

Leslie Grossman.

SOME OF US LEARN OUR success strategies from mentors, teachers, or coaches. Some of us learn them from books. My own success strategy has always included elements of circles of collaboration, but now that I understand how to use them in a more efficient and productive way, I see just how essential they are to success. Christine and I have defined and refined the concept on these pages. It's a work in progress. For us all.

I began building what we've now identified as circles of collaboration by watching my parents in action. They were givers, not only to their children but to the people around them. And in return, people gave to them.

They were New Yorkers who had moved to the rural community of York, Pennsylvania. To them, it felt like a foreign country. Instead of skyscrapers, there were farms. They had no relationships in York when they arrived, but by the time I was four, I noticed we were surrounded by friends and so-called aunts and uncles. Where did these relatives come from? They came from their new community, their circle.

My dad ran his own furniture business and was active in local organizations, including the fire department, where he was a volunteer fireman and later became president of the local Optimist Club. Whenever people needed help, my dad was there. His business was built on his circles.

My mom was a homemaker who created her own circle of collaboration by joining the PTA and the Ladies Auxiliary of the synagogue. She even landed a radio talk show through one of Dad's connections. He needed a new radio program to reach female listeners, and she loved to talk about everything.

My parents' circles became my role models. I mirrored their approach in high school, college, and throughout my career. I observed their give-and-receive dynamic and applied it to my own network. Their approach led to their success and happiness, and it has led to mine.

And now, with a structured framework, my circles have become more intentional, and the results even stronger.

Building New Circles in a New Place

When I moved to Connecticut from New York City during the pandemic, I was excited to be closer to family, but I lacked the day-to-day professional relationships I had relied on for decades. To rebuild, I reached out to the one person I knew in my new state, invited her to lunch, and asked for advice.

Without hesitation, she recommended me for membership in the International Women's Forum, a global organization with a Connecticut chapter for women professionals.

That was two years ago. Since then, I have added some of the incredible people I met there into my circles of collaboration. While I continue to rely on and support the people in my circles in New York, across the U.S., and around the world, I now also have a local core group I can meet for coffee, share ideas with, and collaborate on professional and personal goals.

Creating Collaborative Spaces for Others

A few years ago, I launched the Her Circle Leadership program, a five-week, live (not recorded) collaborative learning experience designed to train coaches in the Seven Tenets of Leadership. This curriculum helps women executives and entrepreneurs advance their careers and grow their businesses through structured collaboration.

What started as a remote program for women across the U.S. became its own circle of collaboration. Long after completing the program, these women continue to collaborate, leverage each other's strengths, and share connections. The program didn't just teach them how to lead. It built a lasting community of leaders.

Expanding My Circles Intentionally

I never stop selectively adding new people to my circles. I actively reach out, explore, and create opportunities for collaboration.

Sometimes, that means making a cold outreach to someone on LinkedIn, but it's always specific to the person I'm approaching and acknowledges why they are someone I'd like to connect with.

Other times, I engage in online communities that align with my interests and goals, including:

- **Entreprenista League.** A network for women entrepreneurs, founded by my former coaching clients Stephanie Cartin and Courtney Spritzer.
- **Innovation Women.** A platform connecting women speakers to events and opportunities.

My circles ebb and flow depending on what I need at different points in my career and life. They are dynamic, constantly shifting as new opportunities arise.

The Power of Collaboration

Perhaps what I love most about my circles is the shared exchange of ideas and knowledge. They challenge my perspectives, push me forward, and provide support when needed.

More importantly, the people in my circles of collaboration genuinely want me to succeed, just as I want success for them. And that is the true magic of collaboration

Chapter 23

Serena Williams: Breaking Up Is Hard to Do.

AH, THE TIGHTROPE WOMEN ATHLETES walk. On the field, or in this case, on the court, they're expected to be fierce competitors. But because of that gender thing that keeps cropping up in all our evolving approaches to how women do everything, they're also expected to be fierce with a tinge of femininity, kindness, or even empathy. Perhaps no female athlete in recent history has drawn more global attention, and criticism, for how she wins than Serena Williams.

And Serena gives us the ultimate lesson in the inevitable course of the development of our circles of collaboration.

One of the most critical elements of Serena's success has been her ability to curate, nurture, and sometimes change her inner circle. It's a process that is as much about her vision as it is about her willingness to make tough decisions.

Serena's vision? To be the number one tennis player in the world without question and for as long as possible. And she brings that same fierce drive to her business ventures. To grow, she has constantly re-evaluated the people around her, making the changes necessary to succeed.

The Evolution of Serena's Inner Circle

Serena's inner circle has been her foundation throughout her career. Her father, Richard Williams, played a pivotal role as her first coach, shaping both her game and her mindset. Her sister, Venus, has been her lifelong partner in the sport, sharing triumphs and trials with unshakable loyalty. More recently, her husband, Alexis Ohanian, has become a steadfast supporter in both her personal and professional life.

Yet, while some members of Serena's circle have been constants, others, including her father, have seen their roles change. Richard Williams is no longer actively associated with her tennis career, a difficult but necessary shift. As Serena grew as a player and a person, the needs of her career evolved, requiring specialized coaching and new perspectives that her father could not provide. And his untethered approach to commenting on all things Serena wasn't always in her best interest.

This decision, like her willingness to change coaches, has drawn criticism from those quick to label her as "ruthless" or "too aggressive." But these labels reveal more about societal bias than about Serena herself.

The Gendered Lens of Criticism

Serena's willingness to change coaches, or even shift her relationship with her father as a coach, when they no longer aligned with her needs, is a testament to her focus and clarity of purpose. Yet, unlike her male counterparts, she has faced intense scrutiny for these decisions.

Take her decision to part ways with her father in an active coaching role. Some framed it as a betrayal of the man who had guided her early success. But the reality was more nuanced. Richard Williams had laid the foundation, but as Serena entered the professional arena, she needed experts who could help her refine and elevate her game.

Contrast this with male players like Novak Djokovic or Andy Murray, who have made similarly significant changes to their coaching teams but were praised for being "strategic" or "focused on winning."

In tennis, and in life, women who assert their needs or make decisive changes are often judged more harshly than men. Serena's experience reflects this double standard. While men are lauded for their relentless pursuit of excellence, women are labeled as "cold" or "ungrateful" for making similar moves.

Changing the Circle to Stay on Top

Serena's changes in her coaching team, and even the shift with her father, have been pivotal to her success. Each coach brought something unique to her game, helping her evolve with the sport.

- Richard Williams laid the foundation, instilling her with discipline and self-belief. His contribution cannot be overstated; without him, Serena might never have picked up a racket.

- Patrick Mouratoglou helped refine her game, leading her to 10 Grand Slam titles during their partnership.
- Others, like Rick Macci and Rennae Stubbs, contributed at different points, offering fresh perspectives and strategies.

Each of these relationships was vital at the time, but Serena's ability to recognize when they had run their course, and to act on that recognition, set her apart.

This wasn't about ruthlessness. It was about staying aligned with her vision of being the best.

Owning the Journey

Serena has made sure that she takes sole responsibility for the journey she's traveling.

Her success isn't just about talent. It's about decision-making, adaptability, and knowing when to change her circles of collaboration to support her next move.

Because breaking up may be hard to do, but staying stagnant? That was never an option for Serena Williams.

Chapter 24

Deborah Martin Chase & Shonda Rhimes: Mentee to Mentor.

WHEN DEBORAH MARTIN CHASE REFLECTS on Shonda Rhimes' meteoric rise, her words carry deep admiration, pride, and a profound sense of partnership. As one of Hollywood's most accomplished producers, Chase has built a legacy not only as a trailblazer for women of color but also as a mentor to countless individuals. Her relationship with Rhimes, which began as a mentor-mentee dynamic and evolved into a powerful partnership, stands out as one of her most rewarding collaborations. Their bond exemplifies the power of mentorship, mutual growth, and the transformative impact of representation in the entertainment industry.

Chase often speaks of Rhimes' rise as no accident but rather the result of visionary talent and relentless drive. "Shonda always had something special," Chase recalls. "You could tell right away that she was a storyteller, not just in her writing but in how she understood people and the dynamics of relationships." She vividly remembers Rhimes' sharp eye for observing the world around her and her ability to transform everyday interactions into compelling narratives. "She was relentless," Chase adds. "Shonda would write and rewrite until the story was perfect.

She has this incredible ability to tap into emotions people didn't even know they had. That's a gift."

Yet Rhimes' success is even more extraordinary given the environment she entered. Chase acknowledges that Rhimes succeeded in a Hollywood that was far from welcoming to Black women storytellers. "When I first started mentoring Shonda, Hollywood wasn't exactly rolling out the red carpet," Chase explains. "But Shonda didn't let that stop her. She found ways to make her voice heard and refused to compromise her vision."

Rhimes' breakthrough wasn't just personal. It was a moment of progress for representation in Hollywood. "Shonda didn't just open doors for herself. She kicked them wide open so that other women, especially women of color, could walk through."

Chase played a crucial role in Rhimes' early days in Hollywood, guiding her as she navigated a challenging industry. "When Shonda worked with me, I could see her hunger to learn," Chase recalls. "She asked smart questions, absorbed everything, and then took it to the next level. My role was to give her the tools, the guidance, and the confidence to trust her own voice."

However, Chase is quick to point out that mentorship is not about dictating a path. "Mentorship is about creating space for someone to find their own way. Shonda always had the talent and drive. All she needed was someone to open the first few doors."

As much as Chase influenced Rhimes, Shonda's success and influence have, in turn, enhanced Chase's career. Their relationship exemplifies the cyclical nature of mentorship, evolving into a collaboration that has enriched both women's legacies. Rhimes has frequently spoken publicly about the critical role Chase played in her journey, which has amplified Chase's reputation as a mentor and industry pioneer. "Hearing Shonda talk about how I helped her always moves me," Chase says. "It's a reminder of why I do what I do. Her success is part of my legacy."

Rhimes' ability to tell diverse, groundbreaking stories is a direct extension of the values Chase has championed throughout her career. "When I see Shonda's work, I see the ripple effect of what we started together," Chase explains. Beyond validation, Rhimes' success has also created new opportunities for Chase. "When Shonda became Shonda Rhimes, the industry started paying attention to stories by and about women of color in a way they hadn't before," she notes. "Her success validated what I had been fighting for all these years."

Chase also draws inspiration from Rhimes. "Shonda's courage to take risks, demand more from the industry, and stay true to her vision is inspiring," she says. "She reminds me of why I got into this business in the first place."

Their relationship has provided moments of reconnection and reflection, especially as Rhimes continues to achieve new milestones. "When Shonda signed her Netflix deal, I thought, 'This is the culmination of everything we've been working toward.' It was a proud moment, not just for her, but for all of us who believed in her."

Key Lessons from Chase & Rhimes

- **Mentorship is an investment.** Chase provided Rhimes with tools and opportunities but allowed her to grow independently, fostering her unique voice.
- **Success is a ripple effect.** Rhimes' achievements reflect Chase's mentorship and amplify her legacy.
- **Paying it forward.** Rhimes has taken the lessons she learned from Chase and applied them to her own mentorship practices, creating a cycle of support that extends far beyond their relationship.
- **Representation matters.** Both women have made it their mission to tell stories that reflect the world's diversity and uplift underrepresented voices.

Together, Deborah Martin Chase and Shonda Rhimes have demonstrated the transformative power of collaboration. Chase provided the foundation for Rhimes to soar, and Rhimes' success has, in turn, validated and amplified Chase's contributions to the industry.

As Chase eloquently puts it, "Shonda's success is my success, and my success is hers. Together, we've shown what's possible when women support women."

Chapter 25

The Inner Circles of Psychoanalysis and Impressionism: Collaboration Fuels Genius.

THERE'S SOMETHING DEEPLY FASCINATING ABOUT the way collaboration fuels genius. We often think of innovation as a solo endeavor. One person's brilliance reshaping the world. But history tells a different story. Whether in science or art, it's the circles of collaboration that spark true breakthroughs. Two of the most compelling examples come from early psychoanalysis and the Impressionist movement, fields that, on the surface, seem disconnected but share a strikingly similar path to innovation.

The Psychoanalytic Circle: Freud, Stekel, and the Birth of a Discipline

In the late 19th and early 20th centuries, Sigmund Freud, Wilhelm Stekel, and a handful of like-minded thinkers met regularly in Vienna, forming the early psychoanalytic inner circle. They gathered in Freud's apartment, a setting that became something of an intellectual battleground, one where ideas were tested, challenged, and refined.

This was not a polite academic seminar; it was a heated, passionate exchange between people determined to redefine human understanding. Freud, as the central figure, guided the discussions, but it wasn't about hierarchy, it was about pushing the boundaries of thought. These meetings, known as the Wednesday Psychological Society, evolved into the Vienna Psychoanalytic Society, and later, into an international movement.

But what made this group special wasn't just their willingness to challenge conventional wisdom. It was the structure of their collaboration:

- **They met consistently.** Collaboration wasn't occasional or informal. It was ritualized.
- **They built on each other's ideas.** Freud had his theories, but Stekel, Adler, and Jung contributed their own interpretations, pushing the discipline forward.
- **They embraced conflict.** Their debates weren't just intellectual exercises; they were often heated, personal, and intense. And while some members broke away (Jung being the most famous example), that friction was part of the process.

Without this circle, psychoanalysis as we know it might not have existed. The act of sharing, debating, and refining ideas collectively turned a revolutionary concept into an enduring discipline. They carefully selected who was in the circle, and they all operated as equals.

The Impressionist Circle: A Rebellion in Paint

At the same time Freud and his circle were dissecting the human mind, another group of disruptors was meeting in Paris. The Impressionists, Monet, Renoir, Degas, Pissarro, Morisot, and others, were redefining what art could be.

Like the early psychoanalysts, they weren't accepted by the mainstream. The Salon de Paris, the gatekeeper of artistic success, rejected their work. Their loose brushstrokes, their obsession with capturing light, and their abandonment of rigid composition were all too much for the art establishment.

So what did they do? They formed their own inner circle. They met in cafés, debated technique, shared feedback, and most importantly, held their own exhibitions. This was a radical move, taking their work directly to the public rather than relying on institutional approval.

The result? Impressionism, once ridiculed, became one of the most influential movements in art history.

Again, the pattern emerges:

+ **They supported each other.** The Impressionists weren't competing. They were elevating each other.
+ **They challenged norms together.** Alone, they might have been dismissed. Together, they created a movement.
+ **They gave each other permission to experiment.** It's hard to be a revolutionary in isolation, but in a group, boldness is contagious.

But isn't this interesting? They were all men. This was not the type of women's circle we have studied over the last few years and have focused on throughout this book. It was men.

How did it work? They were equal in their inner circle meetings. And while we can laugh about how Freud perhaps bossed them around a bit, none of them held the "final" determining decision-making power. They all took the value of what the others contributed and brought it into their individual work.

Chapter 26

Why Do Men Form Collaboration Circles in Creative Fields But Not Business?

BOTH OF THE EXAMPLES FROM the previous chapter, psychoanalysis and Impressionism, show men gathering in intellectual and creative circles to push their disciplines forward. But when we look at collaboration in business, something shifts.

We see fewer tight-knit, idea-exchanging circles among men in business. Instead, business collaboration among men often takes the form of hierarchical networking, mentorship, strategic alliances, boardrooms, but rarely the creative, challenging, peer-driven exchange we see in other industries.

So what does that mean?

One possibility, though not one we've measured with data or extensive research, is that men tend to form collaborative circles in spaces where hierarchy is less defined, where innovation requires breaking the rules rather than enforcing them. In both psychoanalysis and Impressionism, the goal wasn't to climb an existing structure. It was to create something entirely new.

This made us wonder: does the rigid structure of business discourage this kind of collaboration? Does the pressure to compete in a capitalist framework make deep, peer-to-peer collaboration seem risky? And more importantly, what happens when we bring the creative collaboration model into business? What happens when we leave out the chief decision-maker or leader?

What We Can Learn from These Circles Today

The lesson here is clear. Whether you're in art, science, or business, the best ideas don't happen in isolation. True innovation comes from challenging conversations, collective problem-solving, and a willingness to experiment. And perhaps most importantly, equal stature within a collaborative circle provides the best results.

Imagine if we applied the Freud-Monet model to modern business:

- What if business leaders met in creative circles, not just boardrooms, where no one was in charge?
- What if innovation was built on challenging each other rather than simply networking or buying your way in?
- What if, instead of waiting for industry approval, businesses did what the Impressionists did and set their own terms, creating their own markets?

The most powerful collaborations aren't about following the rules. They're about rewriting them. And the best circles? They don't just push ideas forward, they create revolutions.

Chapter 27

Inviting Men Into the Circle of Collaboration.

WE HAVE GIVEN YOU THE history of circles of collaboration and our method for bringing it into your life as a guidepost on your pathway to success. We believe we've made the case for its value.

For centuries, women have instinctively collaborated in circles, spaces where each person has an equal voice and serves as a specialist in their area of expertise. But as patriarchal systems rose to dominance, they disrupted these circles, replacing them with rigid hierarchies where leadership was defined by power, control, and singular direction. These pyramidal structures became the blueprint for patriarchal societies, spreading into corporations, governments, and organizations worldwide.

Yet our collaborative circles never disappeared. That says so much. Women brought them into the places where we had power, like families, communities, and grassroots movements.

What's been missing? A formal introduction into the business world. It's time to change that.

Science confirms what women have always known, that collaboration produces better results. Studies show that simply sitting at a round table fosters more productive discussions, more equitable participation, and better problem-solving. If we are to design a future that works for everyone, the circle of collaboration must expand, and men must learn to fold into this model.

Collaboration vs. Leadership: A Shift in Power Dynamics

One of our co-authors, Christine, proposes a radical reframing. She suggests the word "leader" should no longer define power structures. Its counterpart is not "follower" but "collaborator." Leaders often operate within a framework of command and control, whereas collaborators seek collective success.

If women lead the way by building circles of collaboration in businesses and companies where we have the power to use them, we can challenge the very foundation of patriarchal leadership. Not to take away anything, but to build something better.

What would this mean for men? When success skyrockets under the circle of collaboration, men will face a choice. They can adapt or risk obsolescence. Leadership as we know it, in a pyramid architecture, may become a relic, like typewriters or fax machines, replaced by a new paradigm where success is defined by shared outcomes rather than individual dominance.

But don't mistake collaboration for a lack of power. There is still power, lots of it, but it exists in expertise and collective responsibility, charging the collaborative course toward success.

Bridging the Gap: Bringing Men Into the Fold

We envision a future where men are not excluded but invited into circles of collaboration. Here's how we think this transition could unfold:

Modeling Collaboration

As women create and excel within collaborative frameworks, men will see the tangible results. These include greater innovation, improved workplace culture, and shared prosperity. Evidence of success will encourage them to adopt these practices.

Shared Ownership

Circles of collaboration thrive on shared responsibility. For men accustomed to top-down hierarchies, this shift may feel uncomfortable at first. But with clear roles and mutual respect, the circle provides space for everyone's expertise.

Hybrid Models

A transitional period might involve blending hierarchical and collaborative approaches. For example, a traditional leader might preside over a team but use circle-style methods for brainstorming, decision-making, or project execution.

Expanding Influence

Women who control wealth and resources are uniquely positioned to drive this change. As more women own companies and lead organizations, they can create collaborative environments that attract male allies and showcase the benefits of this approach.

Letting Go of "Leader" Per Se

To fully embrace collaboration, we need to redefine the word "leader" and its baggage of singular authority. Imagine a world where leadership is replaced by facilitation, and success is measured not by who gets credit but by how effectively the group achieves its goals.

When women embrace this mindset, they're not just improving their own organizations. They're redefining what success looks like for everyone.

It's no longer about one person standing at the top of the pyramid. It's about a network of interconnected circles, driving progress together.

What Happens to Patriarchal Hierarchies?

The pyramid structure of patriarchal leadership won't disappear overnight, but it will weaken as circles of collaboration gain momentum.

Companies operating within rigid hierarchies may struggle to compete with those that adopt collaborative models. Employees, both men and women, will increasingly seek workplaces that value their voices and skills.

This isn't about overthrowing men or excluding them. Instead, it's about creating a space where everyone can thrive.

Women's circles have always been a place of inclusion and mutual respect, and men can benefit from this approach, too.

A New Vision for Success

As women step into our power, backed by wealth, expertise, and the collective strength of collaboration, the world will see a dramatic shift in how organizations function.

The question is not whether men can adapt but how quickly they'll recognize the advantages of joining the circle. This is not a call to follow women but an invitation to collaborate with them.

By letting go of outdated notions of leadership, we open the door to a future where success is shared, power is distributed, and innovation thrives. It's time to send the word "leader" out the window and embrace a world built on circles of collaboration.

Let the era of collaboration begin.

Chapter 28

Ready, Steady, Go!

THAT'S IT. IN A NUTSHELL. Two years of debate, study, collaboration, and testing, testing, testing. We are constantly working on our own version of circles of collaboration to fit our personalities, our visions (very different for the two of us), and our changing landscapes as we chart and adjust our course and goals.

That's the thing. Circles of collaboration is a living entity, introduced into an arena surrounded by centuries of rigid structures and deeply ingrained ways of doing things. It's an outlier concept, and we like that about both our book and our method.

Our Vision for Circles of Collaboration

That women all over the world (and men too) start to work it, challenge it, revise it, and share it in ways that work for them.

The true legacy of this book won't be the two of us who put it out into the world. It will be the collaboration of those who read it, use it, and shape it into something even greater.

We hope to hear from you.

And don't be afraid to do the ask if you have questions, challenges, or successes around the method we hold dear.

Christine Merser & Leslie Grossman

Epilogue

A MILLENNIAL WHO WORKS IN marketing for our publisher, Apricity Publishing, read *Circles of Collaboration* in preparation for the book's launch.

After reading, she sat down and decided she wanted to create her own circles of collaboration.

She spent a lot of time working through the vision section and came to a realization. She didn't have a single long-term vision for where she wanted her life to go. Instead, she had many mini-me visions.

"Is that okay?" she asked during a meeting.

Of course. She can approach it in whatever way works for her. Each of us needs to chart our own course in using circles of collaboration as a tool for success. We look forward to hearing how different people approach it.

She loves to travel. She lives to travel. It brings her great joy, fuels her curiosity, immerses her in different cultures, and exposes her to new art and exploration. She takes every opportunity to do it.

Then, she started drawing her circles.

A funny thing happened. She realized that while she often met wonderful people on her travels, she usually lost touch with them afterward.

A few years ago, she went on an equestrian tour through the wine country of France with her mother and ten other travelers. She bonded with a woman whose husband had no interest in that kind of vacation, so she had come alone. At the end of the trip, they promised to keep in touch.

After reading *Circles of Collaboration,* she realized she never had.

Since then, our colleague has moved to Europe, much closer to where this woman lives.

Now, she's gathering the courage to reach out after all this time. She's going to email her, catch up, and perhaps even propose another equestrian trip together somewhere new.

We wanted to share her story, and her circles, not just because it reinforces what we believe to be true about building and working our circles of collaboration for our best lives, but because every person who engages with this approach will ultimately find their own unique way to make their circles work for them.

Stay in touch. *Circles of Collaboration* is on LinkedIn, where we'll continue to share updates as the ideas in this book unfold in real life.

F.P.'s Vision
Life that Involves Travel

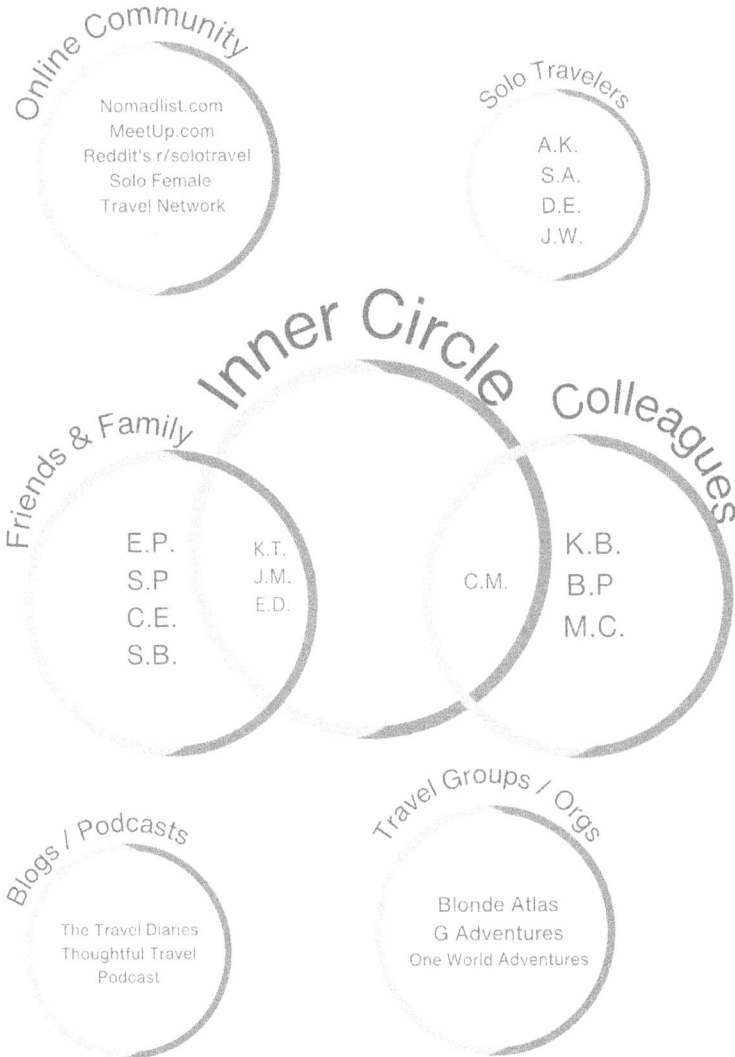

Online Community

Nomadlist.com
MeetUp.com
Reddit's r/solotravel
Solo Female
Travel Network

Solo Travelers

A.K.
S.A.
D.E.
J.W.

Inner Circle

Friends & Family

E.P.
S.P
C.E.
S.B.

K.T.
J.M.
E.D.

C.M.

Colleagues

K.B.
B.P
M.C.

Blogs / Podcasts

The Travel Diaries
Thoughtful Travel
Podcast

Travel Groups / Orgs

Blonde Atlas
G Adventures
One World Adventures

Frances's Circles of Collaboration.

Acknowledgements

WE HONOR THE COUNTLESS CIRCLES of women who, for thousands of years, have gathered in collaboration, holding space for wisdom, strength, and shared purpose, even when society pushed for hierarchy and division. Their quiet perseverance kept this way of community alive, making it possible for us today to grow, nurture, and expand it. Because of them, we have the opportunity to reshape how decisions are made, forging a path toward collective good and the fulfillment of every woman's dreams.

About the Authors

Christine Merser

Christine's journey into understanding the profound impact of gender on every aspect of life began in the 1990s after she became a single mother, launched her marketing and strategy consultancy, and navigated life post-divorce. In 1993, she founded the Women's Resource Center in New York City, dedicated to empowering women through education and advocacy. She has served on numerous boards of directors, including Empower Her Network, which supports the recovery of trafficked women, and Women's World of Backgammon, which she co-founded to increase women's participation in competitive backgammon from 14% to nearly 30% in just three years.

A passionate advocate for women in media, Christine reviews films and television for *Her Screen Thoughts*, offering insights from a female perspective to a devoted audience. She remains committed to amplifying Women in Film's mission to reshape the cultural perception of women in American storytelling.

Christine also advises women philanthropists focused on leveraging their wealth to create meaningful change for women worldwide.

As a sought-after speaker, Christine has addressed audiences across the country on women's evolving roles in business. These interactions revealed how women can harness their innate strengths and unique perspectives to revolutionize corporations and entrepreneurship. Her thought collaboration has been featured in *The New York Times, Newsweek,* and her widely read Substack columns *America Interrupted Dispatch* and *The Voice Inside My Head.*

Christine is also a novelist. Her book, *Flight of the Starling,* follows a middle-aged photographer's journey to the Middle East to rescue her billionaire friend's daughter, who was trafficked decades earlier, transforming from a woman of means into a black ops operator.

With *Circles of Collaboration,* Christine explores the rich history of women gathering in circles, an age-old practice, and how this approach can transform both the journey to success and the outcome. Drawing from history, her own experiences, and those of the many women who have gone before us, she outlines how collaboration, when rooted in an organized approach to the people we gather around us, can drive success, both personally and professionally.

Christine's daughter, Sarah, in her thirties, has already amassed an incredible circle of collaborators, demonstrating the generational growth of the circle theory and its promise for future generations.

Leslie Grossman

For nearly two decades, Leslie Grossman has been a trailblazer in leadership, gender equality, and women's empowerment. An accomplished executive coach, dynamic keynote speaker, and highly regarded researcher, Leslie transforms executives and entrepreneurs alike with her insights and actionable strategies for success.

Leslie made her mark in New York City by founding the Women's Leadership Exchange, the first national conference program for women entrepreneurs and executives. Over its 10-year run, she built a powerful platform that inspired thousands of women to reach new heights in their careers and businesses. Today, as Faculty Director and Senior Fellow of the Executive Women's Leadership Program at The George Washington University Center for Excellence in Public Leadership, Leslie is a thought leader shaping the next generation of women leaders.

Leslie is the author of three impactful books, including her latest, *Start with Vision* (Apricity Publishing). This practical handbook equips women to craft and achieve their personal and professional visions through the 7 Tenets of Leadership: Vision, Presence, Communication, Mindset, Collaboration Circles, Courage, and Confidence. Her innovative framework provides a clear pathway for women to excel at every career stage. Her previous books include *LINK OUT: How to Turn Your Network into a Chain of Lasting Connections* (Wiley) and *SELLsation: How Companies Can Capture Today's Hottest Market, Women Entrepreneurs and Executives* (WPE Press).

Leslie's programs and presentations are uniquely tailored to resonate across diverse settings, including corporate environments, academic institutions, and women's organizations. Whether she's addressing senior executives, college students, or professional networks, or leading workshops online or in person, Leslie's presentations are designed to connect deeply, offering audiences the tools to break barriers, step into leadership, and create a legacy of impact. With her research on women in senior leadership, Leslie offers unparalleled expertise and fresh perspectives.

From running a communications business in NYC to launching a groundbreaking leadership conference and an intensive program for executive women at GWU, Leslie has a track record of transforming ideas into successful movements. Her programs seamlessly adapt to corporate, academic, and organizational contexts, ensuring meaningful impact in every environment.

Leslie grew up in York, PA, raised her family in New York, and currently lives in Connecticut. She is a mom to two successful adults, married to a supportive and patient husband, and a grandparent to four amazing children, two boys and two girls.

* 9 7 9 8 9 8 9 9 0 6 9 4 9 *